Unraveling the "Model Minority" Stereotype

Listening to Asian American Youth

SECOND EDITION

Unraveling the "Model Minority" Stereotype

Listening to Asian American Youth

SECOND EDITION

Stacey J. Lee

Foreword by Christine Sleeter

Teachers College, Columbia University
New York and London

Published by Teachers College Press, 1234 Amsterdam Avenue, New York, NY 10027

Library of Congress Cataloging-in-Publication Data

Lee, Stacey J., 1962–
    Unraveling the "model minority" stereotype : listening to Asian American
  youth / Stacey J. Lee. -- 2nd ed.
    p. cm.
    Includes bibliographical references and index.
    ISBN 978-0-8077-4973-9 (pbk. : alk. paper)
      1. Asian American youth—Education (Secondary) 2. Asian American
    youth—Social conditions. 3. Asian American youth—Ethnic identity. I. Title.
    LC2633.4.L44 2009
    373.1829'95073   2008054827

ISBN 978-0-8077-4973-9 (paper)

Printed on acid-free paper
Manufactured in the United States of America

16   15   14   13   12   11   10   8   7   6   5   4   3   2

Contents

Foreword

Almost thirty years ago I spent eight weeks in Japan. Prior to that time I had not given much thought to my own perceptions of Asians; I probably assumed I had none. I recall that when I stepped out of the airplane in Tokyo International Airport, I had a vivid impression that the airport was filled with people who looked exactly alike. I seemed to see hundreds of people who were small in stature, had black hair, and wore white shirts and navy blue skirts or pants. While I probably would have denied holding stereotypes of Asians before that experience, I did indeed filter the complex and multifaceted reality around me through a very simplified stereotype. Over the next eight weeks I came to know many Japanese people, some quite well. By the time I left, I realized that I had to work to recall stereotypes I had arrived with, since none of them—physical, psychological, intellectual, or attitudinal—fit the highly varied individuals I had come to know. It was an effort to bring the stereotypes to mind, they bore so little relationship to people I had come to know and care about.

When I returned to the United States and arrived in San Francisco International Airport, I experienced another surprise: for the first few minutes, the airport seemed to be filled with white Americans who looked alike! As I recall, I saw an image of good-looking Caucasian people around the age of 25, slender of build, and sporting red and blond hair. Apparently the people of color in the airport were invisible to me at that point; I seemed to see Americans as white. Having grown up with white people and never having considered white people to have any defining characteristics, the experience of seeing a homogeneous mass of white people was a shock. It was also short-lived; my eyes quickly adjusted to the variation among the people who were actually around me.

I learned from this experience that perceptions of people are mediated by categories, images, and words that do not necessarily bear resemblance to real human beings. I have often reflected on this experience and wondered where the images in my head came from (magazines and movies come to mind), and why I was unaware I was carrying them until contact with people in particular contexts triggered them. In both airports, I did not focus on other phenomena around me nearly to the degrees that I focused on people. And I saw but did not see actual people; the people around me triggered images in my head, and it was the images that I saw. In the San Francisco airport, the stereotyped imagery dissipated quickly, but in Japan it took much longer to dissolve.

One direction an analysis of stereotypes can take is to ask the questions: How true is the stereotype, and how can we learn to perceive people more accurately? Generally one can find some individuals who fit the stereotype, although the *stereotype* greatly distorts and oversimplifies even those individuals. Further, it excludes many, many more people who do not fit the stereotype, rendering them invisible or silent. Such an analysis suggests the stereotype can be combated by getting to know various individual people who are members of the group under consideration. As I got to know people in Japan, stereotyped images did indeed recede.

Another direction for analysis, the one taken in *Unraveling the "Model Minority" Stereotype,* is to scrutinize the construction of the stereotype itself: what it means to people, where it comes from, how it is used, and conditions under which it is clung to most tenaciously. David Theo Goldberg (1993) argues that the questions surrounding racial discourse should focus not so much on how true stereotypes are, but on how the truth-claims they offer are a part of a larger worldview, and what forms of action that worldview authorizes.

> In a field of discourse like the racial what is generally circulated and exchanged is not simply truth but truth-claims or representations; these representations draw their efficacy from traditions, conventions, institutions, and tacit modes of mutual comprehension. (p. 46)

Racial truth-claims draw their authority from contexts of human power struggles and exclusion. Such truth-claims, projected through various forms of language and media, authorize and normalize forms of domination and control.

Stereotypes of Asians in the United States shift in substance as the vectors of race relations shift. Once labeled by non-Asians as "inscrutable" and "wily," Asians are now termed "the model minority." Although different in character, both *stereotypes,* like the image I saw when I arrived in Japan, characterize Asians as homogeneous and "Other." The image of the "model minority" on the surface, strikes many people as complimentary. What forms of action could that image authorize that might need to be questioned critically? E. San Juan, Jr. (1992) situates that image in a global context in which the expansion of Western capitalism has resulted in a transfer of wealth from across the globe to an elite, mostly white, minority.

> What the liberal state and the corporate mass media have accomplished is this: a highly selective and distorted privileging of a few successful individuals reduces the diverse Asian population to a monolithic yellow-skinned mass, ignores the large number of disadvantaged underclass . . . , and thus legitimizes the prevailing system of racially based economic inequality underpinning the powerlessness of peoples of color. (p. 135)

The model minority image authorizes flat denial of racism and structures of racial dominance, and silences those who are not economically successful. It also denies and silences Asian America's tradition of militancy and liberation, and a tradition of building solidarity with other oppressed racial groups (Omatsu, 1994).

In this book Stacey Lee examines how young people incorporate, interpret, and make meaning of the "model minority" stereotype in the context of their lived experience in school and community. This book presents a fascinating ethnographic study of a high school in which Lee examines the identities of Asian American students, and the filters through which students of diverse racial groups see and interpret each other. In so doing, Lee examines how the "model minority" stereotype silences many Asian American students, fractures racial groups in the school, and deflects attention away from white racism. Lee also presents a long-overdue portrait of very diverse identities Asian American students construct for themselves.

Lee uncovers four quite different identities that Asian American students construct, and examines what each identity means to them and how these identities interface with the "model minority" stereotype in the broader society, which all of the students are familiar with. She situates these different identities within a highly stratified "pyramid of power" within the school itself, which is exacerbated by the academic competition the school supports. She also situates the school itself within unequal power relations in the community, relations that are crystallized and enacted in sharp relief within the school. In so doing, she offers a powerful critique of an image that many people—Asian and non-Asian—take for granted as positive. She does not, however, oversimplify the complexities of race relations in the school and community. Indeed, she clearly recognizes contradictory choices that Asian American students see themselves as needing to make, and skillfully helps readers to recognize the dilemmas inherent in such choices.

Lee gives voice to the diverse students she met, allying herself most closely with those who identify themselves as Asian Americans. The Asian American students connect themselves with the legacy of struggle against oppression that Glenn Omatsu (1994) contrasts with a growing conservatism in Asian communities today. By critiquing that conservatism as it is played out through the model minority stereotype, Lee invites readers to critically examine the school contexts we create for young people, and to create contexts supportive of equality dialogue, human dignity, and historical consciousness.

—Christine Sleeter,
California State University Monterey Bay

REFERENCES

Goldberg, D. T. (1993). *Racist culture*. Oxford: Blackwell.

Omatsu, G. (1994). The "four prisons" and the movements of liberation: Asian American activism from the 1960s to the 1990s. In K. Aguilar-San Juan (Ed.), *The state of Asian America* (pp. 19–70). Boston: South End Press.

San Juan, E., Jr. (1992). *Racial formations/Critical transformations*. Atlantic Highlands, NJ: Humanities Press.

Acknowledgments

This book started out as my dissertation project many years ago and many people have shaped and challenged my thinking about race and the model minority stereotype since that time. I am especially indebted to Frederick Erickson, Michelle Fine, A. Lin Goodwin, Sara Goldrick-Rab, Carl Grant, Kevin Kumashiro, Joy Lei, Pauline Lipman, Mary Metz, Michael Olneck, Gilbert Park, Xue Lan Rong, Dao Tran, and Lois Weis. A big thanks to Debbie Wei, Ellen Somekawa, and all my other friends at Asian Americans United for fueling my passion for social justice back when I was in graduate school. Many thanks to Mary Jo Gessler for running the department so the rest of us can write and teach. Thanks to the anonymous reviewer for the thoughtful feedback on my proposal for a second edition. Thanks to the folks at Teachers College Press for supporting my work. Susan Liddicoat guided me through the first edition and Brian Ellerbeck helped me think through the details of the second edition. I want to give a very special thanks to Lisa Konoplisky and our family for absolutely everything. And finally, an enormous debt of gratitude goes to all of my former research participants at Academic High. A big thanks to "Dr. Levine" for letting me into his school and thanks to "Xuan," "Young," "Thai," "Kay," "Lee," "Ming," and all the others for letting me into their lives.

CHAPTER I

Asian Americans: The Model Minority Stereotype and the Rhetoric of a Post-Racial America

On June 21, 1989, Academic High School held its graduation ceremony for the class of 1989. In keeping with tradition, Academic High held its ceremony at the Academy of Music building. This beautiful, historic landmark is the home of the city orchestra and the city opera company. Graduation was set for 10:00 a.m. I arrived at 9:00 a.m. and found crowds of graduating seniors and their families spilling over onto the boulevard. I met parents, served as a photographer, and even got included in a few snapshots.

This was to be a big day in Academic High School's history. In the words of the principal, "It was a year of firsts." The principal was alluding to the fact that it was the first year that Academic High had a female valedictorian and the first year that the school had a female senior class president. Thus, this graduation marked the success of coeducation at a school that had resisted admitting girls until the 1980s. For the principal it was a personal success. For many of my Asian American student informants, it was also a year of firsts. For Meng, Pho, Lin, and many others, this marked the first time that someone from their families would graduate from high school in the United States. Thu, Sam, and Grace would be the first in their families to go on to college. After months of fieldwork I considered many of these students to be my friends, and I was happy for them and proud of them. The day seemed perfect, and for a while I began to get caught up in the excitement of the day, forgetting that I was there as an ethnographer.

At 9:45 a.m., I went inside the hall where parents and friends filled the seats. At 10:00 a.m. sharp, the Academic High School orchestra began to play "Pomp and Circumstance," and the faculty, dressed in academic garb, began to file into the auditorium. After the faculty, the graduating seniors began to march down the aisles; the audience began to cheer and cameras began to flash. The auditorium shook with excitement until the procession reached the letter C. With the letter C came the first large group of Asian American students. At that moment the audience suddenly grew silent. It was as if no one cared about the achievements of this group. Suddenly I heard the sound of hissing and booing emerge from the front of the auditorium. My jaw nearly dropped to the ground, and my eyes began to well up with tears. While I was upset for my informants, I also felt personally attacked. Once again, I was reminded that as Asian Americans, we are not always welcomed. After I overcame my initial anger, I realized that this was an ethnographic moment that had to be recorded. Therefore, this event shook me out of the clouds and back to my purpose as an ethnographer.

As I work on the 2nd edition of this book, the graduates of Academic High's class of 1989 prepare for their 20th high school reunion. Although nearly 2 decades have passed since the events of the 1989 graduation, the social and political position of Asian Americans remains remarkably similar. Asian American students are still being positioned as high-achieving model minorities. As in 1989, Asian Americans continue to be held up as exemplars of the American dream of upward mobility through individual achievement. The positioning of Asian Americans as model minorities continues to promote interracial tension between Asian Americans and other groups of color and working-class whites. Finally, Asian Americans continue to be seen as outsiders and foreigners who are potential threats to the fabric of American society. As I argued in the 1996 edition of the book, the events of the 1989 graduation reflect the fact that Asian Americans are simultaneously stereotyped as perpetual foreigners and model minorities. The individuals who jeered the Asian American youth at graduation resented what they perceived to be the overachievement and overrepresentation of Asian American students at Academic High.

The ethnographic study at the core of the book remains unchanged. The focus of the book is still on how the stereotype of Asian Americans as model minorities affected the Asian American students' experiences, their relationships with non-Asians, and their self-defined identities. Asian American students at Academic High divided themselves into four self-defined identity groups: Asian American, Asian, Korean, and New Wavers. Each of the four identity groups had distinct attitudes toward schooling and interracial relationships, and each had a unique response to the model minority stereotype. By examining the impact of model minority stereotype on the students at one school this book highlights the way larger social and political discourses around race circulated and intersected with local school-level practices and beliefs.

Since the publication of the 1st edition of this book there has been a small explosion of published research on Asian American youth and education (e.g., Pang & Cheng, 1998; Park, Goodwin, & Lee, 2001, 2003; Park, Endo, Lee, & Rong, 2007; Weinberg, 1997). Some of this research has focused on the educational experiences of specific Asian ethnic groups thereby focusing attention on the varied educational achievement of students categorized under the Asian American label (e.g., Lee, 2005; Lew, 2006; Louie, 2004; Smith-Hefner, 1999; Thao, 1998; Um, 2003; Walker-Moffat, 1995; Zhou & Bankston, 1998). Some researchers have worked to explicitly challenge the model minority stereotype by highlighting the concerns of Asian American students who fail to achieve model minority standards (CARE, 2008; Lee & Kumashiro, 2005; Li, 2005; Li & Wang, 2008; Olsen, 1997; Pang, Kiang, & Pak, 2003; Walker-Moffat, 1995). In recent years the debate surrounding the model minority stereotype has received the attention of mainstream institutions. The College Board, for example, collaborated with researchers from New York University to produce a report challenging the assumptions of the model minority stereotype (CARE, 2008). My understanding of the academic and social experiences of the Asian American students has benefited greatly from this proliferation of literature. Ultimately, my decision to work on a 2nd edition of this book stems from my belief that the specific experiences and identities of the Asian American youth at Academic High still offer a unique glimpse into the way the model minority stereotype operates in the everyday lives of Asian American students.

In this edition of the book my goals are to explore the continuing significance of the model minority stereotype in the early 21st century. I have significantly revised Chapter 1 and Chapter 6 of the book, but have left Chapters 2–5 untouched. In Chapter 1 I will trace the historical development of the stereotype and examine the continuing social and political impact of the stereotype on Asian Americans and on other groups of people of color. I will illustrate the way in which the stereotype has evolved under the social and political context of neoliberalism. I will also include a discussion of the way the Immigration and Nationality Act of 1965 and the refugee resettlement have shaped the Asian American population. The following questions frame the discussion: How has the model minority stereotype evolved in recent years? When and under what social, political, and economic circumstances are images of Asian Americans as model minorities mobilized? How are images of Asian Americans related to images of other racialized minority groups? How does the stereotype mask diversity within the Asian American category? In Chapter 6 I will reconsider the ethnographic data collected in 1989 in light of recent social science literature on immigrant and minority education, and the research on Asian Americans specifically.

ASIAN AMERICANS IN THE
BLACK AND WHITE DISCOURSE ON RACE

In the United States the dominant discourse on race focuses on blacks and whites. Race relations, racial inequality, and conceptualizations of race are all understood largely in terms of the black-white racial paradigm (Hune, 1995). The dominance of the black-white racial paradigm reflects the fact that historically blacks and whites were the two largest racial groups. Furthermore, the institution of slavery and the ongoing racial subordination of blacks have led most Americans to equate blackness with minority status. Within the black-white racial paradigm, whites are understood to be dominant and blacks are understood to be subordinate, and racial inequality is framed in terms of the differences between the two groups. In education, for example, the achievement gap has been framed primarily in terms of the underachievement of blacks relative to whites. In recent years dominant discussions of race have included Latinos, but the black-white racial paradigm shapes these conversations as well (Hune, 1995; Park & Park, 1999).

Although neither black nor white, Asian Americans have been understood within the black-white racial paradigm, and depending on the historical period Asian Americans have been likened to blacks or whites (Okihiro, 1994). According to legal scholars, Asian Americans have been treated as "constructive" blacks throughout much of the history of the United States (Ancheta, 2003; Wu, 1995). For example, legal scholar Angelo Ancheta points out that in the mid-19th century and the early 20th century the courts classified Chinese Americans as blacks, and that Asian Americans "endured many of the same disabilities of racial subordination as African Americans—racial violence, segregation, unequal access to public institutions and discrimination in housing, employment, and education" (p. 5).

Although Asian American experiences have been influenced by the black-white racial paradigm, it would be a mistake to conclude that the black-white racial paradigm can sufficiently account for the racialized experiences of Asian American. Once again, the work of legal scholars is helpful in highlighting the unique ways in which Asian Americans have been racialized (Ancheta, 2003; Chang, 1993; Matsuda, 1991; Wu, 2002). Ancheta (2003) and Chang (1993), for example, argue that the subordination of Asian Americans has occurred largely by casting Asian Americans as foreigners (i.e., not Americans) who are unable and unwilling to assimilate into mainstream American culture and society. Cast as perpetual foreigners, Asian Americans have often found their patriotism and loyalty to the United States in question. Throughout history, as victims of nativistic racism Asian Americans were subjected to the most severe and restrictive immigration and naturalization policies faced by any racial group (Ancheta, 2003; Chang, 1993; Lee, 1989). During World War II, nativistic racism led to the internment of Japanese Americans (Ancheta, 2003; Chang, 1993). The rhetoric of some of the most outspoken anti-immigrant activists of today reveals a deep racism, including anti-Asian sentiment (Brimelow, 1995). Recent studies suggest that many non–Asian Americans continue to see Asian Americans as essentially foreign. In 2001 the Committee of 100, a nonpartisan, national Chinese American organization, commissioned a study on American attitudes toward Chinese Americans and other Asian Americans. The study revealed that 25% of Americans hold "strong negative attitudes" toward Chinese Americans. These negative attitudes included the perception that Chinese Americans are clannish, and the fear that Chinese Americans were more loyal to China than to the United States. Furthermore, 28% of those surveyed believe that the growth of the Asian American population is "bad for America" (versus the 31% who believed that the increase in the Hispanic population was bad for America). Significantly, the study found that the majority of non-Asian Americans could not distinguish between different Asian ethnic groups. Thus, we can assume that the negative attitudes toward Chinese Americans extend to other Asian groups as well (Committee of 100, 2001).

The perpetual foreigner stereotype affects the lives of all Asian Americans. While European immigrants are accepted as authentic Americans soon after their arrival in the United States, 3rd-, 4th-, and even 5th-generation Asian Americans are often perceived to be foreign (Tuan, 1998; Waters, 1990). I have yet to meet an Asian American who has not had to field questions regarding his or her origins. When I tell people that I was born in California, most non-Asians respond by asking yet another question: "But where are you really from?" Recently when I explained to a white acquaintance that my mother was born in Greenwood, Mississippi, and that my father was born in Boston the individual asked me whether my parents were Asian or American. This seemingly innocent question reveals the assumption that Asianness and Americanness are mutually exclusive. In schoolyards across the United States Asian American students are taunted by the following words: "Go back to your own country!" Like the questions regarding our origins, these taunts remind Asian Americans that they are not seen as legitimate members of the United States. In her research on multiple-generation Asian Americans, Tuan (1998) found that her research participants believed that the term "American" was reserved for whites, and that as Americans of Asian descent they would always be hyphenated Americans.

Significantly, the positioning of Asian Americans as perpetual foreigners has played a central role in excluding them from dominant discussions of race. In other words, because Asian Americans are viewed as foreigners (i.e., not American) they are not understood to be central to the American discourse on race. Legal scholar Frank Wu argues, "Asian Americans have been excluded by the very terms used to conceptualize race. People speak of 'American' as if it means 'white' and 'minority' as if it means 'black.' In that semantic formula, Asian Americans, neither black nor white, consequently are neither American nor minority" (Wu, 2002, p. 20). Significantly, when Asian Americans are brought into the dominant discussions of race it is usually to identify Asian Americans as model minorities. Here, Asian Americans' success is used as proof that equal opportunity exists. In the process they become "honorary whites," a status that denies the fact that Asian Americans experience racism.

THE MODEL MINORITY
STEREOTYPE AS A HEGEMONIC DEVICE

The term "model minority" first appeared in the popular press in January 1966 in William Peterson's *New York Times* article, "Success Story Japanese American Style," in which he praised Japanese Americans for not becoming a "problem minority." Within the year, *U.S. News & World Report* published an article lauding the success of Chinese Americans. The author wrote, "At a time when it is being proposed that hundreds of billions be spent to uplift Negroes and other minorities, the nation's 300,000 Chinese Americans are moving ahead on their own—with no help from anyone" ("Success Story," 1966, p. 73). The article went on to praise the good citizenship of Chinese Americans and the safety of Chinatowns. The fact that the stereotype first appeared in the middle of the Civil Rights movement was no coincidence. Just months before the Peterson article was published in the *New York Times*, the Voting Rights Act of 1965 was passed and the 1965 Watts riots occurred. Critics of the model minority stereotype have argued that the emergence of the stereotype at this moment in history represented the attempts of the status quo to silence the charges of racial injustice being raised by African Americans (Osajima, 1988; Sue & Kitano, 1973; Wu, 2002).

It was also during the mid-1960s that social scientists began to talk about poverty as a cultural phenomenon. Poor people were described as living in a culture of poverty that shaped their actions and behaviors in ways that trapped them in poverty. Significantly, poverty became associated most closely with urban blacks during this period (Katz, 1990). Blacks became associated with the culture of poverty after the 1965 controversial Moynihan Report argued that the weaknesses of the black family threatened the black community's chances for social mobility. Since then blacks have been equated with urban blight, cultural deficiency, and dysfunctional families. Commenting on the way in which the Moynihan Report was interpreted by the dominant society in 1965, Fultz and Brown (2008) explain "the report seemed to imply that the 'disorganization' of the Black family was one of many 'pathologies' (e.g., female-headed households and male unemployment) internal to the black community rather than responses to sociocultural constraints" (p. 862). In contrast to the representation of blacks during this period, Asian Americans were heralded as model minorities with strong families and good cultures. Indeed, the rhetoric of the model minority stereotype emphasized the role of Asian culture and families in the success of Asian Americans.

The prescriptive nature of the model minority stereotype is striking in both the Peterson article and the *U.S. News & World Report* piece. Chinese Americans and Japanese Americans were singled out as good citizens and good minorities precisely because they were seen as quiet, uncomplaining, and hard-working people who achieved success without depending on the government. According to these authors the success of Asian Americans proved that all groups could achieve the American dream through hard work. That is, Asian Americans as model minorities were used to exemplify the achievement ideology. Victor Bascara (2006) describes the centrality of the model minority stereotype to the achievement ideology like this: "The notion of a model minority also places that minority into a developmental trajectory as its best fruition. Members of that minority are a testament to the success of the incorporative capacities of the United States, politically, economically, and culturally. The model minority has become integrated, modernized, and civilized" (p. 5). African Americans were implicitly being told to model themselves after Asian Americans. While Asian Americans were held up as shining examples of hard work and good citizenship, African Americans were positioned as loud, complaining, and lazy. Put differently, there can be no model minority without the concomitant lazy, underachieving black "other." Thus, as a hegemonic device the model minority stereotype maintains the dominance of whites in the racial hierarchy by diverting attention away from racial inequalities and by setting standards for how minorities should behave.

During the 1980s the model minority stereotype reached beyond Chinese and Japanese Americans to include Southeast Asians as well. In his analysis of the evolution of the model minority stereotype, Osajima (1988) asserts that, although the popular press began to recognize the potential negative implications of the model minority stereotype during the 1980s, it continued to portray Asian Americans as exemplary minorities who gain success through sheer effort and determination. The cover story for

Time's August 31, 1987, issue illustrates Osajima's point. The article, "The New Whiz Kids: Why Asian Americans Are Doing So Well, and What It Costs Them," lauded the academic achievement of Asian American students (Brand, 1987). It included stories of Southeast Asian refugees who overcame extreme obstacles to achieve academic success. In the author's words, "By almost every educational gauge, young Asian Americans are soaring" (p. 42). Once again, Asian Americans are depicted as brave, silent, and long-suffering people. The implicit message is that individual effort will be rewarded by success and that failure is the fate of those who do not adhere to the value of hard work. During my research at Academic High, one of my earliest clues to the significance of the model minority stereotype for Asian American students' identities was that Asian American students repeatedly mentioned that they had read the aforementioned "Whiz Kid" article.

In the traditional family values rhetoric espoused by neoconservatives during the 1990s, Asian American families were held up as exemplars of old-fashioned, traditional, good families. Not insignificantly, the traditional Asian family was contrasted with the stereotypical dysfunctional black family headed by a single black mother on welfare (Hamamoto, 1992; Palumbo-Liu, 1994). In the 1992 riots that followed the Rodney King verdict, the conservative press depicted Korean Americans as hardworking, self-made immigrants whose property was threatened by the unlawful anger of black America. Here, Korean Americans became stand-ins for white, middle-class America (Palumbo-Liu, 1994). Asian Americans were once again being used as hegemonic devices to support notions of meritocracy. The sad irony, however, was that even while Asian Americans were being used by the mainstream press to support dominant group interests, Asian immigrants were largely abandoned in their time of need (Cho, 1993).

During the 1990s Asian American students, portrayed as high-achieving model minorities, also became central to the debates surrounding higher education admissions. Opponents of affirmative action positioned Asian American as victims of race-based admissions policies. According to anti–affirmative action activists, Asian Americans were model minorities who were losing seats in universities and colleges to less-qualified beneficiaries of affirmative action policies (CARE, 2008; Kumashiro, 2008; Takagi, 1992). The rhetoric of color blindness and meritocracy were central to the assaults on affirmative action in which affirmative action was characterized as preferential treatment for the undeserving. When the University of California regents disbanded affirmative action in 1995, anti–affirmative action activists asserted that Asian American student populations would increase (Ancheta, 2003). Here, the interests of Asian Americans were clearly articulated as being at odds with the interests of blacks and Latinos. California's Proposition 209, which banned all affirmative action in public employment, public education, and public contracting, was passed in 1996. Significantly, while anti–affirmative action advocates positioned Asian Americans as model minorities in their assault on affirmative action, the passage of Proposition 209 was made possible in part by nativist sentiments directed at both Latinos and Asian immigrants (Ong, 1999).

Throughout the 1990s the image of Asian American students as model minorities was used in attacks against other race-based policies. In these discourses, minority status was equated with underachievement and underrepresentation, which in turn led to the deminoritization of Asian Americans (Lee, 2006). In the 1995 case of Ho, Wong & Chen v. SFUSD affirmative action and desegregation became conflated in the public mind (Robles, 2006). In this lawsuit a group of Chinese Americans challenged the San Francisco School District's desegregation policy, which required ethnic and racial caps at all public schools. Specifically, the plaintiffs focused on the differential admissions requirements for various ethnic and racial groups at Lowell High School, the district's best high school (Ancheta, 2003; Robles, 2006; Wu, 2002). One of the remarkable things about this case is that the Chinese American plaintiffs embraced the model minority stereotype in their fight against the city. In her analysis of the Ho case, Robles argues, "The Ho lawsuit is a case through which we can examine how Chinese Americans have utilized the stereotype of the Asian American Model Minority to transform themselves into victims of race-based policies within this neoconservative, colorblind social and political context" (2006, p. 4). While the Ho case pit Chinese Americans against African Americans, Wu's (2002) analysis of the case suggests that whites, not blacks, were the greatest beneficiaries of the district's desegregation policy. Wu asserts, "Neither side noticed the affirmative action for whites. As the largest group competing with Chinese Americans, whites benefited the most from the limit on Chinese Americans" (p. 142). Significantly, Wu's analysis suggests that the model minority stereotype effectively diverted attention away from whites. By buying into the image of Chinese Americans as model minorities, the Chinese American plaintiffs and their supporters implicitly bought into the parallel stereotypes of blacks and Latinos as underachieving and undeserving beneficiaries of the district policy. Thus, this case demonstrates the hegemonic power of the model minority stereotype in protecting the interests of the dominant group. The Lowell High case is particularly interesting for our understanding of race relations at Academic High because both schools hold special positions within their respective cities. In both schools, Asian Americans as model minorities are positioned against African Americans.

The attacks on affirmative action and other race-based educational policies during the 1990s reflect the cultural, racial, and social politics that have emerged under neoliberalism during the last few decades. In theory and in practice, neoliberalism is marked by free markets, privatization, economic deregulation, and the decline of social welfare policies (Harvey, 2005; Kumashiro, 2008; Lipman & Hursh, 2007). Neoliberal discourses celebrate individual freedom, competition, meritocracy, and achievement. In his influential text on the rise of neoliberalism, Harvey (2005) writes, "The assumption that individual freedoms are guaranteed by freedom of the market and of trade is a cardinal feature in neoliberal thinking" (p. 7). Within the neoliberal framework, each individual is conceived of as an entrepreneur responsible for his or her own welfare (Lipman & Hursh, 2007).

Significantly, neoliberalism assumes that all individuals can participate in the market free from structural barriers to individual achievement (Kumashiro, 2008). In short, neoliberal discourses support the rhetoric of postraciality, which assumes that race no longer matters. According to postracial logic, we live in a color-blind society in which the goals of Civil Rights era have been accomplished. Despite the rhetoric of neutrality, objectivity, and fairness, neoliberal policies have been found to heighten inequality (Harvey, 2005; Whitty, 1997). Within the color-blind and postracial discourse of neoliberalism, any continuing racial and economic inequality is understood to be the result of individual pathology (Lipman, 2008; Robbins, 2004). Social welfare programs are therefore implicitly understood as handouts to the undeserving. Thus, neoliberal conceptualizations of race and of individuals in the free market helped to set the stage for attacks on affirmative action.

The assault on race-based educational policies, including affirmative action, represent an alliance between neoliberal forces and neoconservatives who decry what they see as the decline of standards (Apple, 2004). According to neoliberals and neoconservatives, affirmative action is preferential treatment, which inhibits the freedoms and rights of qualified individuals. These anti–affirmative action activists capitalized on the language of meritocracy, fairness, and color blindness in their fight to end affirmative action. Not insignificantly, the same anti–affirmative action activists who embraced the rhetoric of color blindness were willing to embrace race consciousness when they positioned Asian Americans as victims of affirmative action (Ancheta, 2003). Again, the message was that Asian American success proves that there are no racial barriers to achievement.

Neoliberal educational policies focus on market solutions such as privatization, choice, standardized testing, and accountability (Apple, 2004; Burch, 2009; Dillabough, Kennelly, & Wang 2008; Lipman & Hursh, 2007). Within this context schools have increasingly come to reflect and perpetuate the logic of the market, and to prepare students for the market (Apple, 2001; Lipman, 2004). Lipman describes the state of education under neoliberalism: "Their hegemonic project has succeeded in redefining education as job preparation, learning as standardized skills and information, educational quality as measurable by test scores, and teaching as the technical delivery of that which is centrally mandated and tested. By defining the problem of education as standards and accountability they have made simply irrelevant any talk about humanity, difference, democracy, culture, thinking, personal meaning, ethical deliberation, intellectual rigor, social responsibility, and joy in education" (p. 181).

The stereotypical high-achieving Asian American student who studies computer science or engineering is seen as ideal in this context, whereas other students, including many Asian Americans, who struggle academically or choose to pursue other fields are viewed as less desirable and less valuable. Although advocates of market-based educational policies suggest that competition will increase opportunities for all students, there is growing evidence that the policies leave some students behind (Lipman, 2004; McNeil, 2000; Whitty, 1997). As schools have become increasingly competitive, there are distinct winners and losers. According to performance on standardized tests, Asian American students may appear to be winners in these educational contests. As I will discuss in the next section, however, the aggregate data that suggests that Asian American students are doing well masks the difficulties faced by some Asian American groups.

The model minority stereotype persists into the early 21st century without any signs of disappearing. In 2006, *New York Times* columnist Nicholas Kristoff heralded the model minority success of Asian American students. The continuing dominance of the model minority stereotype reflects the fact that the stereotype continues to support the rhetoric of the achievement ideology. Asian Americans as model minorities are the ideal neoliberal subject—motivated, self-sufficient, and successful. The model minority success of Asian Americans is interpreted as evidence that markets are neutral and color-blind. Similarly, Asian Americans as model minorities represent the ideal neoconservative subject—traditional, family-oriented, and hardworking. The stereotypical image of the Asian family, with the strict patriarchal father, the dutiful mother who lives solely to guide her children's education, and the obedient children who do well in school, serves the rhetoric of traditional family values espoused by neoconservatives. As in the Civil Rights era, the model minority stereotype pits Asian Americans against other groups of people of color and supports the rhetoric of meritocracy. At Academic High I found evidence of tension between Asian Americans and African Americans at Academic High, but I also discovered evidence of resistance to the model minority construction of race. For example, there were a few Asian Americans and African Americans who attempted to build a coalition of racial minorities to deconstruct white dominance. I will highlight both consensus and resistance to the hegemony discourse of the model minority stereotype.

The continuing visibility of the model minority stereotype can also be attributed to the fact that some Asian Americans have actively worked to perpetuate the model minority image, which was apparent in the Ho case. Notably, there exists a split among Asian American scholars between those whose work challenges the model minority stereotype and those whose work supports the stereotype (Li & Wang, 2008). At Academic High, many Asian American students willingly embraced the model minority stereotype. Their embrace of the model minority representation was partially motivated by the fact that the characterization of Asian Americans as model minorities seems positive and even flattering when compared with the stereotypes of other racial minorities. Furthermore, Asian American students at Academic High were often rewarded with teachers' praise and high grades for performing like model minorities. In their attempts to live up to the model minority standards, many Asian American students censured their own experiences and voices. Self-silencing and the uncritical acceptance of the model minority stereotype represent Asian American consent to hegemony. Although the majority of Asian American students at Academic High School spoke proudly of being stereotyped as model minorities and even engaged in the self-silencing of their experiences, there were Asian American students who actively resisted the conditions of the model minority stereotype.

Finally, the stereotype has persisted because there appears to be some evidence to support the idea that Asian Americans are successful. At Academic High some of the most successful students were Asian Americans. However, the success of these students masked the growing academic struggles of other Asian American youth. By describing Asian Americans as model minorities, the diverse and complex experiences of Asian Americans remain hidden. The issue of diversity within Asian America will be addressed in the next section of this chapter.

INSIDE ASIAN AMERICA: THE HIDDEN DIVERSITY

Asian Americans are one of the fastest-growing groups in the United States. According to the 2004 American Community Survey, the Asian population was estimated to be 13.5 million, or 4.7% of the U.S. population (U.S. Census Bureau, 2007). In 1990, the year I concluded my research at Academic High, Asians made up 2.8% of the U.S. population (Reeves

& Bennett, 2003). The tremendous growth of the Asian population in the United States is due in large part to continuing immigration. The 1965 Immigration and Nationality Act abolished the national origins quota, which had been in effect since 1924. The restrictive national origins system passed in 1924 had significantly limited the number of Asian immigrants and favored immigrants from Europe. The 1965 Immigration Act gave priority to "family reunification," which meant that U.S. citizens and permanent residents could sponsor relatives to come to the United States as immigrants. Preference was also given to immigrants who were professionals, scientists, and in fields where there were labor shortages. Since the passage of the 1965 Immigration Act record numbers of immigrants from Asia and other non-European countries have entered the United States. While many of the Asian immigrants who came in the 1970s and 1980s were highly educated professionals, subsequent waves of immigrants have included poorer and less educated immigrants from Asia. With the end of the Vietnam War in 1975, Southeast Asians began to enter the United States as political refugees. The first wave of Southeast Asian refugees included educated professionals (e.g., middle-class Vietnamese), and the later waves included those from poorer, rural backgrounds with fewer transferable skills. The pattern of immigration has resulted in a bimodal distribution of social class within the Asian American category (CARE, 2008; Hing, 1993). It is important to note that most of the highly successful Asian American students at AHS were the children of the earlier wave of post-1965 immigrants, or first wave of Southeast Asian refugees.

A highly heterogeneous group, the "Asian" category includes people who trace their ancestry to East Asia, Southeast Asia, and the Indian subcontinent. Asians are diverse in terms of ethnicity, culture, social class, religious affiliation, language background, educational attainment, and generation in the United States (Lee & Kumashiro, 2005). Recent data show that Chinese, Asian Indians, and Filipinos were the largest Asian ethnic groups in the United States (U.S. Census Bureau, 2007). The lumping of various Asian ethnic groups into one category, however, masks significant diversity. Much of the aggregate data on Asian Americans give support to the model minority image. The results of the 2004 American Community Survey, for example, revealed that the median income of Asian households ($56,200) was higher than that of non-Hispanic white households ($48,800) by approximately $8,000 (U.S. Census Bureau, 2007). With respect to education, in 2004 approximately 85% of Asians age 25 or older were high school graduates, and nearly 50% had a bachelor's degree or higher. Among non-Hispanic whites age 25 or older, 89% were high school graduates and about 30% had bachelor's degrees or higher (U.S. Census Bureau, 2007). Data on Asian Americans disaggregated by ethnicity, however, reveal a more complicated picture. While Asian Indians, Chinese, Japanese, and Koreans are doing well economically and educationally as groups, Cambodians, Hmong, and Lao suffer relatively high rates of poverty and low rates of educational attainment. Data from Census 2000 reveal that 53.3% of Cambodians, 59.6% of Hmong, and 49.6% of Lao age 25 or older have less than a high school education. During this same period, almost 30% of Cambodians, 37.8% of Hmong and 18.5% of Lao lived under the poverty line (Reeves & Bennett, 2004). Because many of the more successful Asian ethnic groups represent the largest Asian ethnic groups, their success masks the concerns and struggles experienced by smaller Asian ethnic groups.

There is mounting evidence that social class and parental education is correlated with educational achievement and attainment among all Asian American students (CARE, 2008). According to a recent national report on Asian American education, students with parents who have graduate-level educations score over 100 points higher on the SAT verbal section than their peers who have parents with less than a high school diploma. Similarly, those from families with parental incomes over $100,000 scored over 100 points higher on the SAT verbal section than students from families with incomes below $30,000 (CARE, 2008). As noted earlier, Southeast Asians experience high rates of poverty and low rates of educational attainment. At the University of California–Berkeley, where Asian and Asian American students make up 41% of the undergraduate population, Southeast Asians represent but a small fraction of this population (Um, 2003).

Studies point to the many barriers faced by Southeast Asian students in their pursuit of education (Lee, 2005; Ngo & Lee, 2007; Um, 2003; Walker-Moffat, 1995). In addition to struggles related to poverty, Southeast Asian students have also been found to lack access to the social capital central to negotiating educational systems (Lee, 2005; Um, 2003). Many Southeast Asian American students have difficulty mastering academic English, a fact that suggests that many public schools lack the qualified staff to work with English language learners (Um, 2003). Furthermore, Southeast Asian students, particularly Hmong, Cambodians, and Lao are often stereotyped by teachers as gangsters and held to low expectations (Lee, 2005; Um, 2003). Commenting on the racial stereotypes faced by Southeast Asian students, Um (2003) asserts, "Southeast Asian Americans are often regarded in binary extremes. On the one hand, they are frequently lumped together with other Asian American groups and viewed as the 'model minority,' with no serious educational challenges or experiences of discrimination. On the other extreme, they are depicted as an irreparably traumatized community of welfare dependents, high school dropouts, and delinquents" (p. 11).

Recent research suggests that even among Asian ethnic groups known for high levels of educational achievement there exists significant variation in social class that affect opportunity and achievement (Lew, 2006; Li, 2002; Louie, 2004; Verma, 2008; Wong, 2008). Class bifurcation is particularly significant within the Chinese immigrant community with many highly educated professionals from Taiwan and Hong Kong and a growing number of poor immigrants from the Fujian Province in China (CARE, 2008; Kwong, 1987; Louie, 2004). Political scientist Peter Kwong (1987) referred to the highly educated immigrants as "uptown Chinese" and those from poor backgrounds employed in low-skilled jobs in Chinatowns as "downtown Chinese." Louie's (2004) study of Chinese American college students examines the different educational trajectories of "uptown" versus "downtown" Chinese. While students from both working-class and middle-class backgrounds reported that their parents held high educational aspirations for them, social class had profound affects on the quality of K-12 schools they attended, and the level and quality of parental involvement. The educated, middle-class Chinese immigrants in Louie's study settled directly into suburban communities with good public schools. Furthermore, they were able to use their resources to provide their children with the advantages associated with middle-class childrearing (Lareau, 2003). By contrast, the working-class immigrants in her study lived in ethnic enclaves in New York City and had limited resources to navigate the educational system. Lew's (2006) comparative study of high-achieving Korean American high school students and Korean American high school dropouts reveals the class bifurcation in the Korean immigrant community, and the way that social class affects access to important social capital necessary for negotiating education. Significantly, the dropouts were from working-class and poor families who were outsiders to the ethnic social networks that benefited middle-class families.

Despite the diverse educational realities of Asian American students, too many educators and educational policy makers assume that Asian American students are high-achieving model minorities, and rely on aggregate data that support the model minority stereotype. Significantly, No Child Left Behind (NCLB) requires that data on students be disaggregated by race, but does not require that data be disaggregated by ethnicity. Therefore, the needs of low-achieving Asian American students are ignored because Asian Americans as a racial group are performing above the standards (Li & Wang, 2008). Aggregate data on Asian American student performance on the Massachusetts Comprehensive Assessment System (MCAS), for example, suggests that Asian Americans are doing well, but school districts with high concentrations of Southeast Asian students have higher numbers of Asian Americans who receive failing scores than districts with predominately Chinese and South Asian students (Pang, Ki-ang, & Pak, 2003).

An examination of the data on English language learners provides further evidence that some Asian Americans are struggling and failing in our schools. Recent data show that 24% of Asian American students are English language learners, and that Asian Americans make up 12% of all English language learners in the United States (AALDEF, 2008). English-language learners are performing significantly below native English speakers on standardized tests used in compliance with NCLB (Men-ken, 2008). Educational researchers and advocates have argued that tests designed for native English speakers are not appropriate for assessing English language learners. According to Menken (2008), "These tests are first and foremost language proficiency exams, not necessarily measures of content knowledge" (p. 4). In one study on the experiences of Asian American students under NCLB the authors discovered that Asian Ameri-cans who are English language learners are being pushed out of some schools because "of fear that ELLs will score low on NCLB-mandated standardized tests" (AALDEF, 2008, p. 8).

Thus, there is growing evidence that some groups of Asian American students (e.g., low-income immigrants, English language learners, South-east Asian Americans) are struggling in our schools. Within the current edu-cational context that emphasizes testing and accountability these students are particularly vulnerable to educational failure, but their specific concerns are hidden in the aggregate data that marks them as model minorities.

In addition to silencing the diverse experiences and concerns of Asian Americans, the model minority stereotype implicitly denies Asian Ameri-can experiences with racism. Here, the success of some Asian Americans is used to support the idea that Asian Americans do not face racial barriers. However, the everyday lives of Asian Americans demonstrate that Asians are the victims of both blatant racial violence and more subtle forms of racism (Chou & Feagin, 2008; Rosenbloom & Way, 2004). Recently, Asian American community groups have been calling attention to the stories of Asian American youth being the victims of anti-Asian bullying and vio-lence. Some youth advocates assert that the stereotypes that Asian Ameri-cans are high achieving and noncomplaining (i.e., model minorities) make them targets of violence. One particularly infamous case involved Lafay-ette High School in Bensonhurst, New York, where Chinese and Pakistani immigrant youth were repeatedly the targets of anti-Asian violence. In 2004 the Federal Justice Department determined that Lafayette school of-ficials deliberately ignored the "pervasive" harassment of Asian American students by their non-Asian peers (AALDEF, 2005). Research on Asian American education suggests that some Asian Americans are, in fact, investing in education as a way to overcome racial barriers (Louie, 2004; Sue & Okazaki, 1990; Tuan, 1998). In other words, Asian Americans are turning to education as an adaptive strategy in response to racism. Ironically, when Asian American students are successful they are often met with racial anxieties about the overrepresentation of Asians. The booing and hissing directed at the Asian American students during Academic High's 1989 graduation are but one example of this kind of racism.

THE SITE: ACADEMIC HIGH SCHOOL

Academic High School is a public high school located in a major city on the East Coast, north of the Mason-Dixon line. As a special-admit school, Academic High accepts students from throughout the city on the basis of standardized test scores and grades. During the period of my research there were more than 110 teachers on the faculty, and many held advanced degrees. The curriculum included standard academic offerings as well as a course in Asian Studies and one in Hebrew. At the time I entered the school there were 2,050 students enrolled at Academic High. The racial breakdown of the student population was 45% white, 35% black/African American, 18% Asian American, and 2% other. The 356 Asian American students at the school represented a range of social class backgrounds and ethnicities. I chose Academic High as my research site because I believed the diversity of the Asian American population would enable me to observe a range of intra-Asian interactions and a range of identity groups.

Even before I ever set foot on the grounds of Academic High School, I heard from a variety of people in the city that Academic High was "different," "special," and "better" than the other high schools in the city. Teachers from other public schools and community members told me that Academic High students were "smarter" and "nicer." Upon entering Academic High for the first time, I was immediately impressed by how the students were free to simply wander the halls. At other high schools in the city there were strict rules against students being in the halls during class periods, and students who broke those rules were treated like petty criminals. When I entered the main office, I was struck once again by how different Academic High seemed. While most other high school offices were dreary places that were painted an institutional green or beige, Academic High's office was lined with student artwork.

When I met Dr. Benjamin Levine, the principal of Academic High, he described Academic High students as being "the nicest kids in the world." When I was introduced to Dr. Rafferty, the teacher of English for Speakers of Other Languages (ESOL), he proudly asserted that Academic High was an intensely academic institution that had been named one of the best high schools in the nation. The idea that Academic High is a special institution pervades the Academic High experience and plays a significant role in race relations among the students.

While Academic High certainly has a unique culture and history, it does share important similarities with other special admissions public high schools in large urban school districts in the Northeast, Midwest, and California. To a certain extent all of these schools are perceived to be jewels in otherwise troubled school districts. As such, admissions are highly competitive, and many of these schools have been plagued by controversy surrounding the racial makeup of the student populations. As noted earlier, the case of Lowell High School in San Francisco illustrates the way Asian Americans, positioned as model minorities, have become central to the debates surrounding race and admissions.

NOTES ON METHODS, POSITIONALITY, AND REPRESENTATION

Prior to entering the field in January 1989 I was not particularly interested in the model minority stereotype. My original research question involved Asian American students' responses to pan-ethnic categorization. My focus was on whether students from various Asian ethnic backgrounds embraced a pan-ethnic identity as either Asian or Asian American. Specifically, I was interested in how social conditions within the school shaped student responses to pan-ethnic identity. Shortly after entering the school the model minority stereotype emerged as a theme. At first teachers, administrators, and students simply referenced the high achievement of Asian American students. Over time, I discovered that the stereotype masked the variation in achievement among Asian American students, and was being used against underachieving African American students. I mention my early research focus here in order to make more transparent the evolution of this research project, and to highlight the centrality of the model minority stereotype at Academic High.

The primary fieldwork for this research was collected for my dissertation between January and June 1989. I spent an average of 4 days a week at Academic High. During my time at the school, Dr. Levine, the principal, allowed me significant freedom to wander around the school. I observed classes, ate lunch with students and staff, attended sporting events, extracurricular activities, and two proms; I also served as one of two adult supervisors for the girls' badminton team trip to the Great Adventure amusement park. I took extensive hand written fieldnotes of my observations and informal conversations with faculty, staff, and students. These notes appear throughout the book. I interviewed Asian and non-Asian students, as well as members of the faculty and staff. During the course of my research, I had regular contact with approximately 82 Asian American students at Academic High, and I conducted semistructured interviews with 47 of these students. The semistructured interviews with Asian American students were audiotaped, and the quotations that appear in this book are verbatim transcripts of these interviews. Semistructured interviews with white and African American students were also audiotaped and transcribed. I did not audiotape interviews with faculty and staff because most appeared to be uncomfortable with being taped, but I did take written notes. In addition to fieldwork in the school, I followed students into their communities. My visits to a youth center, the mall where students congregated, and to the homes of a few participants helped me understand more fully the lives of these youth.

Throughout the summer of 1989 I continued observing and interacting with eight Asian American student informants as they participated in various youth activities sponsored by community organizations. During the 1989–90 school year I continued to have contact with informants through phone conversations. My contact with Academic High ended on June 13, 1990, when I attended Academic High's 1990 graduation ceremony. Throughout the book I use pseudonyms for all my informants. Because of the importance of ethnicity, I made every attempt to give informants pseudonyms that match their ethnic backgrounds. In a few cases, students selected their own pseudonyms. I also pay attention to giving gender-specific names and titles. I use pseudonyms for the school and the city as well. Although people familiar with public high schools on the East Coast may be able to identify the school, I use a pseudonym to shift the focus away from this particular school and to redirect the focus toward public schools in general. I can't stress enough that it would be unfair and wrong-headed to isolate this school for any "blame." The findings—positive and negative—were only discovered because Dr. Levine gave me access to the school and the teachers and students allowed me into their lives and told me their stories. While particular events and people are unique to this school at a particular historical moment, I want to stress that the questions and concerns raised by the data speak beyond the school. Hegemonic ideas about race, and the model minority stereotype in particular, resonate beyond the walls of Academic High. In fact, I would argue that Academic High represents a microcosm of the larger society, and that the racial dynamics at Academic High reflect racial conditions in the United States.

In places in the book my voice will appear alongside those of my informants. I will make my presence transparent when it is most relevant to understanding how my identity and voice influenced the research process. In this way, I hope to call attention to the relationship between self/researcher and other/informant, thereby "working the hyphen," a term coined by Fine (1994). Fine asserts that, by "working the hyphen" in qualitative research, "researchers probe how we are in relation with the contexts we study and with our informants, understanding that we are all multiple in those relations" (p. 72). Prior to embarking on my fieldwork at Academic High I had done a substantial amount of reading on researcher identity, and I was convinced that while researcher identity matters, all research is partial and located. I assumed that my race, ethnicity, and gender might influence the way students, teachers, and administrators would respond to me. I assumed that my prospective Asian American informants would focus on my ethnicity and/or race, and see me as Chinese, American-born Chinese (ABC), Asian, or Asian American. I was interested in whether my Asian American informants would view me as an insider (i.e., fellow Asian American) or as an outsider, and I decided to use their interpretations of my identity and their responses to me as data.

Upon entering the school I found that students were, in fact, curious about my ethnic background. Most students asked the following kinds of questions: What are you? Are you Chinese? I quickly learned that I had to make special efforts to develop contacts within the Korean American student population because of their tendency to maintain strict in-group and out-group boundaries. Although the Korean-identified students always saw me as Chinese and therefore an outsider, they could identify with my middle-class status, and many aspired to attend the Ivy League institution where I was a graduate student. As a result of my relationship with the Korean students, I began to understand the significance of social class in their identities.

In addition to my ethnic/racial identity and social-class identity, I discovered that my gender, age, American-born status, and position as a graduate student influenced how students reacted to me. At the time of my research, I was in my late 20s, and in retrospect I realize how my age helped to facilitate relationships with the youth. Although many of my Asian American informants remarked that anyone over 21 was old, many also asserted that I looked young because I was Asian. I became a confidante to many students, who shared their stories about romantic flirtations, family problems, and future plans with me. Students regularly joked around with me and teased me. Some Asian American students referred to me as an older sister or aunt. As a graduate student, I gained some status in the eyes of the high-achieving students and in the eyes of some Korean-identified students. These students asked me about my educational background and about my personal experiences applying to college.

While my status as a graduate student helped me in my contacts with high-achieving students, it made it difficult for me to gain the acceptance of the low-achieving Asian Americans who were expressing resistance to schooling. These students, known as the new wavers, saw me as part of the authority structure and viewed me with suspicion. Eventually I was able to gain their trust, and some of them began to see me as a potential homework assistant. In looking back over my fieldnotes I now recognize that I had better luck establishing trust with new wave boys than girls.

One of my most interesting findings in regard to my identity was that most Asian American students did not think of me as an American even once they learned that I was born and raised in California. To many students of Asian descent, only white people were considered to be Americans. Although many of my informants had difficulty accepting that I was American, some of my informants also found my behavior to be un-Asian. Dorrine Kondo (1990), a Japanese American anthropologist, encountered similar reactions from her Japanese informants in Japan, who found her to be both Japanese and not Japanese. One of my informants found my habit of bringing my own lunch in a brown paper bag to be very "American." In an almost accusatory tone, he said, "You are like an American—you bring your own lunch. Only Americans bring their lunch!" When I asked him why Asians did not bring their own lunches, he told me a story about a time in elementary school when he had to bring his lunch to school because his class was going on a field trip. He said, "You know, I brought some kind of Asian food, and the kids made fun of the way it looked and smelled." He asserted that he thought most Asians had been teased for bringing Asian food. This student's story helped me to recognize the way some Asian American students had been silenced by the ethnocentric behavior of their non-Asian peers. It also made me aware of the political nature of food, and the relationship between food and identity. Finally, the interaction made me aware that these students were watching me and trying to decipher me, just as I was watching them. According to this student, my actions were decidedly un-Asian.

My identities also influenced the ways that I related to and responded to what my research participants said and did. In the beginning, I hid my attitudes, politics, and beliefs from both students and adults. I made every attempt to appear neutral. Whenever students asked me what I thought, I attempted to redirect the conversation back to them. By taking this position, I was able to establish relationships with a variety of students from often-conflicting camps. Eventually, however, I found that my silence was not neutral. Because I am an Asian American adult and because some of the students teased me about being like their sister or aunt, I realized that students might see me as a role model. Thus I feared that my silence in the face of racist, sexist, homophobic, and classist remarks might be interpreted as sanctioning. On the other hand, I did not want to force my opinions and ideas on my informants because I believed that I would then be guilty of silencing my informants in much the same way that the stereotypes and institutional structures had silenced them. In the end, I adapted an approach whereby I attempted to challenge students and encourage them to examine their racism, sexism, homophobia, and so forth (Lather, 1986; Roman & Apple, 1990). I should note that I do not think I ever managed to change a single student's opinion. One student, Thai (see Chapter 5), regularly approached me to debate controversial issues because he believed these interactions helped to sharpen his rhetorical skills.

In reading over my data nearly 20 years later, I'm struck by the likelihood that my ethnic and racial background coupled with my graduate student status may have led some of the teachers and administrators at Academic High to see me as a model minority, and that this may have prompted them to share their negative attitudes toward African American students with me. Although I remember being somewhat shocked and disturbed by the racist assumptions shared by some of the teachers, I generally chose to listen without comment. I hoped that through collecting and sharing their stories I would be able to provide insight into how the model minority stereotype was used in the service of the status quo. In writing about the politics and ethics of conducting research on racism with racist participants, Vaught (2008) argues for relational responsibility in which the words of racist participants are placed within the larger cultural system. Some readers have suggested that my representation of Dr. Levine was particularly critical, verging on harsh. It was not my intent to demonize Dr. Levine; rather, it was my goal to illustrate how his position as the principal, his white racial identity, and his politics shaped his understandings of the school. Furthermore, I would argue that his actions and words reflect the larger system in which belief in the achievement ideology leads to blaming the victims.

As I was writing the dissertation I asked a few student participants whether they wanted to read chapters, but most declined and/or were only interested in reading where they were quoted. Over the years I have received generally positive feedback from Asian American readers who believed that I accurately captured some of the diversity and complexity of Asian American experiences. One important exception to the generally positive feedback has been from some Korean American readers who have voiced concerns regarding my representations of the Korean-identified students. In particular, some of these individuals have expressed concern that I portrayed Korean students as being ethnocentric and elitist. The concerns expressed by these critics made me realize that I likely did not do enough to put the identity formation of Korean-identified into a larger context. It is important to note, for example, that compared to other Asian ethnic groups Koreans are relatively culturally homogenous. While there are many Chinese dialects, there is one Korean language. Research suggests that the cultural homogeneity of the Korean American population allows for and encourages Koreans to socialize with other Koreans and to maintain the Korean language and various aspects of Korean culture (Min, 1991). As Jamie Lew's work on Korean American youth demonstrates, however, there is significant class variation in the Korean American community that affects access to social networks. Group solidarity among Korean American students at Academic High was enhanced by the fact that most of the Korean American students at the school were from the middle/merchant class. I will do more to situate the identity formation of Korean-identified students into the larger literature on Korean Americans in the updated conclusion to the book.

The concerns raised by these Korean American individuals raise important questions and concerns regarding the politics of representation. As a racialized minority, it is understandable that some members of the Korean American community would be sensitive to representations that might perpetuate stereotypic ideas about their group. My own mother was critical of the 1st edition of this book when it was published in 1996 because she didn't like my critique of the model minority stereotype. Like other Asian Americans of her generation, she is concerned with how Asian Americans are perceived by the dominant society, and she views the model minority stereotype to be relatively positive compared to the more overtly negative stereotypes that she remembers from her days growing up in Mississippi in the 1940s and 1950s. Writing and research are always political acts, and this work is not an exception. My original goals for this book, and my goals today, are to unravel the workings of the model minority stereotype. I believe, as I did in 1996, that this is an important political act.

A NOTE ON THE POLITICS OF IDENTITY LABELS

Throughout the book I will use the term "Asian American" when referring to students of Asian descent as a group. The specific Asian ethnic groups included in this study were Cambodian, Chinese, Korean, Lao, and Vietnamese. Although there were a few American-born Asians at the school, most of the Asian American students at Academic High were immigrants from China, Hong Kong, Taiwan, and Korea or refugees from Cambodia, Laos, and Vietnam. It must be emphasized that the term "Asian American" is my term and not the term used by the majority of Asian American students at the school. With the exception of a small group of students who identified themselves as Asian American, most students of Asian descent did not identify with the label. Interestingly, most of the students had trouble with the American part of the label, not the Asian part. In fact, with the important exception of Korean-identified students, most students of Asian descent shared a pan-ethnic/racial identity as Asians.

Originally, the dominant group imposed the term "Asian American" on people of Asian descent because they saw Asian Americans as a homogeneous group (Espiritu, 1992; Lowe, 1991). Other examples of pan-ethnic categories created by the dominant group include Latino/Hispanic, Native American/Indian, and African American/black (Cornell, 1988; Espiritu, 1992; Keyes, 1981; Trottier, 1981; Waters, 1990). During the 1960s Asian American activists representing different ethnic groups joined forces to fight for equal rights and embraced the term "Asian American" as a political term (Espiritu, 1992; Lowe, 1991; Omi & Winant, 1986). In writing about the politics of an Asian American pan-ethnic identity, Lowe (1991) warns against "essentializing" Asian America and silencing the diversity of Asian American experiences:

> A politics based on ethnic identity facilitates the displacement of inter-community differences—between men and women, or between workers and managers—into a false opposition of "nationalism" and "assimilation." (p. 30)

In writing about the different groups, I have attempted to pay attention to the ways in which gender, social class, sexual orientation, and other variables influence an individual's experience and his or her identity.

ORGANIZATION OF THE BOOK

This book centers on the experiences of the four Asian American identity groups at Academic High School. The following questions emerge and reemerge throughout the book:

- What do Asian American student identities tell us about the formation of ethnic/racial identity?
- How does the variation in Asian American student identity contribute to our understanding of the literature on immigrant minorities (e.g., Gibson, 1988, 1991; Ogbu, 1987, 1991)?

- How did the model minority stereotype influence Asian American student identity?
- What identities were encouraged and discouraged by the school?
- How did the model minority stereotype influence race relations?
- What influence did the school have on race relations?

In Chapter 2, I introduce the four self-defined Asian American identity groups. I place attention on the similarities and differences among the groups and on the relationships among the groups (i.e., intra-Asian dynamics). A central theme concerns the way Asian American students from various ethnic backgrounds responded to the "Asian pan-ethnic" categorization. My original assumption prior to conducting the research was that Asian American students would form pan-ethnic/racial identities in response to negative experiences with non-Asians. In other words, I viewed ethnic groups as "communities of interest" who organize around common concerns and experiences (Espiritu, 1992). This chapter focuses on students who embrace pan-ethnicity by identifying as Asian and/or Asian American and on students who identify solely with their specific ethnic group. Other issues considered are the salience of social class and gender to identity.

Chapter 3 turns to stories of Asian American student achievement. Voices of high- and low-achieving students are highlighted. The focus is on how students' identities influenced their attitudes toward schools and their achievement. Questions to be considered include: What were their perceptions regarding future opportunities? How did they view the role of schooling in their lives?

Chapter 4 deals with how race relations at Academic High are constructed. The focus is on how school policies influenced race relations. We hear about race from the perspective of African American, white, and Asian American students. This chapter examines how school forces and the model minority stereotype influenced race relations at the school.

In Chapter 5, we hear about race from the perspective of African American, white, and Asian American students. This chapter examines how school forces and the model minority stereotype influenced race relations at the school.

In Chapter 6, the major issues in the book are revisited. In this new version of Chapter 6 I will discuss the themes of the book in light of more recent literature on Asian American experiences in education.

As a whole, this book attempts to underscore the insidious ways in which the model minority stereotype affects Asian American students.

CHAPTER 2

What's in a Name?
Asian American Identities at
Academic High School

May 4, 1989—This was a really busy day. After school I ran back
and forth between the girls' badminton game and the Korean
Students' Association meeting. One minute I would be in the
bleachers with several of my Asian-identified informants cheering
on the badminton team, and the next minute I would be sitting
among my Korean informants listening to them discuss election
procedures. It was a little frustrating because I felt like I kept
missing things in both places, but I had to show up in both places
so that it would not appear as if I were favoring Koreans over
Asians or vice versa.

When I first arrived at Academic High School, several teachers informed
me that the Asian American students had split themselves into two
groups: Koreans in one and all other Asians in another. On the surface,
the teachers' observations seemed to be accurate. I found that, with the
exception of most Korean students, who identified solely as Korean,
Asian American students at Academic High shared a pan-ethnic identity.
However, while they shared a pan-ethnic/pan Asian identity, they did
not make up a single identity group but divided themselves into three
subgroups: Asian, Asian new wave, and Asian American. Thus the students I termed Asian American at Academic High divided themselves
into four self-defined identity subgroups (i.e., how they referred to themselves and to each other): Korean-identified, Asian-identified, Asian new
wave-identified, and Asian American-identified. Identity groups usually
translated into social groups or subcultures, but membership in a subculture was also influenced by academic achievement and academic tracking. For example, high-achieving students often crossed identity groups
to socialize with other high-achieving students. Since students' identities

were fluid and not static, movement among identity groups did occur. Finally, it should be stressed that I am not arguing that each of the 356 Asian American students at Academic High belonged to one of these groups. Rather, I am suggesting that these are broad groupings that speak to the reality of most Asian American students at Academic High.

In this chapter I describe the four Asian American identity groups and the individuals who belonged to the groups. We hear how the students defined themselves and whom they defined as "other." Emphasis is on the relationships between and among the different Asian American subgroups. Attention is also given to the relationship between an individual's identity and his or her responses to the model minority stereotype.

KOREAN-IDENTIFIED STUDENTS

The majority of the Korean students at Academic High were immigrants who had come to the United States when they were in elementary school or middle school. Scholars have coined this the 1.5 generation; however, I did not observe Korean students referring to themselves in this manner (E.-Y. Kim, 1993; J. F. J. Lee, 1991). The English-language skills of the Korean students varied from those who spoke English like native English speakers to those who experienced difficulties with English and were enrolled in the ESOL program. Most of the Korean students were from middle-class/merchant family backgrounds, and most lived on the north side of the city, which has a large Korean immigrant population. As noted earlier, most Korean students identified themselves solely as Korean and not as Asian or Asian American.

In their attempts to maintain a distinctly Korean identity, Korean-identified students distanced themselves from all other Asian Americans. These students marked their distance by emphasizing the differences between Koreans and other Asian Americans. During a conversation in the music room (recorded in my fieldnotes for February 2, 1989), five Korean-identified students spoke of the differences between Koreans and other Asian Americans:

> *Brian Sung*: For some reason Koreans don't mix [with other Asian Americans]. I don't know, maybe it's us . . .
> *Jane Lee*: I don't think that we dislike each other; it's just that we are different people, so we don't really relate to each other.
> *Lisa Kim*: We think of ourselves as being more superior.
> *(The group laughed and nodded in agreement.)*
> *SL*: So, Koreans don't hang out with other Asians?

Peter Choe: No . . . well, some do, but not as a group.

SL: Do you think there are any similarities between Asians and
     Koreans?

Sophie Lee: I don't find any similarities . . . they [other Asians] seem
     so different to me.

Although the Korean-identified students saw differences between Koreans and other Asian Americans, they often grouped all other Asian Americans into one category. Lisa Kim said, "Other Asians all seem to dress, act,
and look alike. I can't tell the difference." As quoted above, she also suggested that Korean difference equaled Korean superiority. The notion of
Korean superiority was echoed by other Korean-identified students. For
example, during an interview Linda Park made this comment about other
Asian Americans:

> It's like I think of Koreans and then all others . . . I guess Koreans
> think of ourselves as more superior than they are. When I think of
> Asians, I think of non-Koreans . . . I mean, I just don't like them at
> all. I find them hideous. I wouldn't want to talk to them.

Although Korean-identified students thought of themselves as being different from all other Asian Americans, non-Asian students and teachers
often lumped Koreans together with all other Asians.

Social Class as a Marker of Difference

Underlying conversations regarding Korean difference and superiority
was a conversation about social class. Korean-identified students asserted
that they were better than other Asian Americans because they were from
higher social-class backgrounds than most of the Southeast Asians. Espiritu
(1992) noted that differences in social and economic class have historically
inhibited the development of pan-ethnic identity among Asian Americans.

During my interview with Linda Park referred to above, I got my first
clue to the significance of social class for Korean identity. After Linda
described Asians as being "hideous," I was on the verge of blowing my
ethnographer's poise and expressing my outrage. With some effort, I
managed to maintain my composure, and I asked Linda whether or not
she knew what my ethnic background was.

Linda: Yeah, you're Chinese.

SL: How did you know that? I mean . . . the last name Lee can be
     almost anything.

Linda: Well, I knew you weren't Korean and anyway, you look Chinese.

SL: Given what you think about Chinese people, I'm surprised you agreed to an interview with me.

Linda: Well, if people are polite, I will talk to them. You asked me nicely. Anyway, you are different than the other Asians. You are more educated, more middle-class.

Linda and the other Korean-identified students found me to be acceptable because they perceived me to be "successful enough." Throughout my fieldwork I felt ambivalent about their "acceptance" of me. As an ethnographer, I was more than happy that they allowed me to gather their stories. Another part of me, however, was uncomfortable with the fact that their "acceptance" of me was based on elitist notions. Yet I feared that if I challenged their ideas regarding other Asians, I would be removed from my privileged position as an "acceptable" Chinese person.

Korean-identified students used clothes as a marker of class difference. Lisa Kim put it rather directly when she said, "We [Koreans] dress better [than other Asians]." These Korean-identified students explained that, while other Asians were "new wave," Koreans were "preps": Other Korean-identified students simply said that they thought that other Asians were "tacky." I learned that new wave–style clothes were generally purchased in inexpensive Chinatown stores and in the mall near Chinatown, while preppy clothes were generally purchased in suburban shops and department stores where the white, middle-class students shopped.

Young Hun Pak explained that many Korean students got their attitudes about Korean superiority and social class from their parents.

They [Korean parents] hate people on welfare because they think they're sponging off the U.S. They think you [should] come here so that you can help yourself and the U.S., not to take their money. You shouldn't come here to ruin the U.S., and that's what they think the Vietnamese and Cambodians are doing.

Korean parents distanced themselves from Southeast Asians because they believed that many Southeast Asians received public assistance and they did not want to be associated with people who might be perceived as welfare sponges. This kind of distancing, also known as disidentification, has historically been practiced by Asian groups who did not want to suffer the consequences of being mistaken for the targeted Asian group (Espiritu, 1992; Hayano, 1981). For example, during World War II, Chinese Americans disidentified themselves from Japanese Americans for fear that they, too, might be accused of disloyalty to the United States (Espiritu, 1992; Takaki, 1989). Korean parents disidentified themselves from other Asians because they did not want Koreans to be blamed for draining the economy and for getting special help from the government. They were intent on representing themselves and other Koreans as hardworking and successful immigrants. Korean students told me that they and their parents were proud of being represented as model minorities. They resented all Asians who risked destroying the model minority image for them. They had, in other words, consented to the hegemonic discourse of the model minority stereotype.

Although I did not gather systematic data on the backgrounds of the Korean students' families prior to immigration, there are obvious differences between Koreans and Southeast Asians. Perhaps one of the biggest differences is that Koreans came to the United States as immigrants and Asians from Vietnam, Cambodia, and Laos came as refugees. Studies have suggested that many Korean immigrants in the United States come from urban, Christian, and educated backgrounds (Light & Bonacich, 1988). Unable to find jobs in their chosen professions, many Korean immigrants became self-employed merchants. Koreans have established their own extended business networks that provide start-up money for businesses (Light & Bonacich, 1988). Most of the Korean students at Academic High reported that their parents were merchants. On the other hand, the Southeast Asian refugees represent an economically and culturally diverse group of people. Differences in the economic status of the refugees are generally related to the date of immigration. The majority of those who are economically successful belong to the group who came to the United States around 1975, during the first wave of immigration; the poor and working-class refugees came later (Rumbaut & Weeks, 1986). At Academic High there were refugees from a range of economic backgrounds. Some Southeast Asian students at Academic High reported being on public assistance, while others had parents who worked in restaurants, in factories, or on farms, and still others had parents who owned small businesses.

Despite the differences between Koreans and Southeast Asians and despite the fact that Korean-identified students made efforts to disidentify themselves from Southeast Asian students, as pointed out earlier, many non-Asians did not recognize the differences and saw all Asians as one homogeneous group. For instance, some non-Asian students believed that Koreans received special public assistance from the government to open stores, and this misunderstanding fueled resentment toward Koreans and other Asians. Teachers also grouped Koreans together with other Asians.

For example, Jane Lee complained to me that Mrs. Marpole, a white woman who taught standard English, had asked her to help Phum Ng with his English homework. According to Jane, Mrs. Marpole had suggested that she would be a good person to help Phum since they were both Asian. Jane was insulted by the suggestion that she, a Korean, might have anything in common with an ethnic Chinese person from Vietnam. Although Jane was upset by this, she did not express her objections to Mrs. Marpole. However, she did express her discontent to me and to Phum. Korean-identified students like Jane responded to ethnic lumping by further distancing themselves from other Asian Americans.

Korean Students' Association

One of the most obvious examples of how Korean-identified students distanced themselves from other Asian Americans was that Korean-identified students refused to participate in functions sponsored by the Asian Students' Association (ASA), and even broke away from the ASA in order to form the Korean Students' Association (KSA). The ASA approached the KSA to participate in joint projects, but the KSA declined their offers. It is important to note that Korean students at other area schools also tried to form separate clubs. For example, the Korean students at the all-girls public high school in the city tried to form their own Korean club, but the administration there refused to sponsor the club since the school already had an Asian students' club. The school's administration did not see the need for a separate Korean club because they believed that the Korean students could simply join the Asian Students' Association. The school's decision to deny support to a Korean club reflected what Espiritu (1992) refers to as institutional ethnic lumping. Members of Academic High's KSA invited the girls from the neighboring school to join their KSA because they believed that "Koreans should stick together."

Members of the KSA are all of Korean descent. Although the active membership consisted of between 20 and 30 students, members considered all Koreans to be unofficial members. In fact, some Korean students spoke of being pressured by KSA members to attend meetings. Kay Row described the difficulty she faced from her Korean peers when she dropped out of the KSA in her sophomore year:

> I got a very negative response, like people said "Are you ashamed of being Korean?" Things like that really bothered me. . . . In fact, I am really proud of being Korean. I have nothing against Korean people.

Kay reported that she had dropped out of the KSA because she wanted to define her own identity separate from the larger Korean community.

She referred to this as her "identity crisis." Kay's experience points to the role of peer group pressure in getting Korean students to conform to a particular image of being Korean. Despite Kay's experience, it is important to note that the KSA always welcomed new Korean members and rewelcomed former members. Membership in the KSA is first and foremost about being Korean. Kay eventually rejoined the KSA and became an officer during her senior year.

Although Academic High's school rules required that all student clubs maintain an open policy to all students, the KSA got around these rules by making their meetings inaccessible to non-Koreans. For example, rather than advertising the dates, times, and places for meetings, as was the practice of other student clubs, KSA members often depended on word of mouth to advertise meetings. As one student said, "A lot of times, instead of putting the meetings in the daily bulletin, we'll just tell people when we see them. You know, like when I see a Korean in the halls, I'll say, 'Hey, club meeting today.'"

The annual semiformal banquet for KSA students was the culminating event of the year for the club. While the ASA and the KSA both held annual banquets, the two events were very different and represent the difference in the clubs. Traditionally, the ASA held their banquet at a Chinese restaurant in Chinatown. The ASA banquet was open to all members and free to those who helped at a bake sale or another fundraising event. The KSA held a semiformal banquet at an expensive center-city hotel. Tickets to the KSA banquet were $60 per couple. As one member put it, "The idea behind the banquet is to have an event like the prom." The banquet was almost an exclusively Korean event because, as David Kim said, "If you ask an American girl, Filipina girl, Chinese girl. . . . She might say 'yes, but I don't think she'd feel comfortable because it's all Korean." It is interesting to note that David places the blame for exclusion on the non-Korean girls.

One of the most significant factors in making the KSA an exclusively Korean club was that the club focused on activities outside of the school rather than on activities inside the school, the way other clubs functioned. Academic's KSA had contact with Korean student associations throughout the city and the surrounding suburbs. KSA members told me that over the last two years a network of 12 Korean student clubs had organized a talent show, an indoor sports competition, and an outdoor sports competition. During the spring semester, the KSA participated in an indoor sports competition with 10 other Korean clubs. The cost of renting the gym was $2,000. The cost of the gym rental was partially paid by tickets to the event: Each participant paid $6 to play on a team, and observers paid $3. The Korean Association, an adult community organization, agreed to pay for the balance.

Learning American Ways

The Korean-identified students' attempt to distance themselves from other Asians was often motivated by their efforts to get closer to white people. Korean students explained that their parents instructed them to socialize only with Koreans and "Americans." Peter Choe said, "When I first came to U.S., they said I should get . . . should hang out with American kids so I could get Americanized. So, I hang out with American kids." When I asked Peter to define what he and his parents meant when they used the term *American,* he and his Korean-identified friends responded in unison with, "white! Korean parents like whites." Korean parents believe that "learning American ways" is the key to success and that their children can learn "American ways" from their white peers.

In order to get closer to whites, Korean-identified students often imitated what they considered to be white American behavior. These students recognized that not all whites have equal social status, and they targeted the more socially prestigious groups as models. In particular, they chose to imitate most closely the white, upper-middle-class students often called "Edgewood types" (referring to the name of an upper-middle-class enclave on the west side of the city). These white students, like the ones Eckert (1989) calls "jocks," were the socially popular, academically good students who were active in school activities.

As noted earlier, the Korean-identified students imitated the preppy style of clothing worn by the "Edgewood types." They also tried to participate in the same activities, eat at the same restaurants, and listen to the same music. For example, through watching the "Edgewood types" and other upper-middle-class people, the Korean-identified students recognized tennis and skateboarding as elite sports. Several ninth-grade boys took up skateboarding because, in their words, "it's a white boy sport." With the price of skateboards being upwards of $100, the term *white boy* seems to imply "middle-class white boy." In addition to "learning American ways," Korean students were encouraged by their parents and other Korean adults to accommodate the dominant group.

Dual Identity

Although Korean parents encouraged their children to learn "American ways" and to accommodate the white majority, the adults also encouraged Korean youth to maintain connections to Korean traditions and people. Korean-identified students stated that their parents wanted them to "remember that we are Korean." Within the Korean community the adults established an elaborate network of business, religious, and social organizations to support Korean connections. Korean students reported that their parents all seemed to know one another. Young Hun Pak, an Asian American–identified student of Korean descent, said this:

> You go into a store, and they see a Korean and give you a discount. It's like, "Oh, I know your mother," or "I know your father. Tell them to come in sometime." They don't care how young or old you are. It's close knit. . . . To everyone else they're closed off.

According to Young, the simple act of going into a Korean-owned store served as a reminder of her Korean identity. The adult networks spawned the establishment of Korean youth networks. For example, many Korean students reported knowing each other through Korean Christian church groups.

Some Korean students complained that the tight-knit nature of the Korean community made them feel as if they were always being watched. Students reported that they were careful about what they did or said around Korean adults because news of inappropriate behavior had a way of getting back to their parents. Similarly, in her study of Punjabi immigrants in California, Gibson (1988) found that community gossip functioned to keep young people from deviating from expected behavior.

At Academic High, Mrs. Kyung Clark, the faculty advisor for the KSA and a teacher in the music department, assumed the job of watching over the Korean students. A Korean immigrant who was married to a white man, Mrs. Clark was the only Korean teacher at Academic (also the only Asian American teacher). Many of the Korean students knew Mrs. Clark from the Korean church. Korean students looked to Mrs. Clark as an adult advisor, and within the music department Clark's office was seen as a hang-out for Korean students.

Mrs. Clark encouraged her Korean students to speak Korean when they were among Koreans. Most Korean students spoke Korean when they were in her office, and KSA members often spoke to each other in Korean during meetings. The few non-Korean Asians in the instrumental music department said that they often felt uncomfortable and excluded because Mrs. Clark "just starts talking to the Korean kids in Korean like we're just not there." Solomon (1992) reports that West Indian students in Canada use the Rasta dialect to keep white students and school authorities out of their business and to secure power for their group. Korean-identified students at Academic used the Korean language for a similar purpose. Use of the Korean language served to keep other Asian Americans at a distance and to keep things among the Koreans. Korean-identified students who were less fluent in Korean would often lapse into English, but they were quickly teased into speaking Korean.

Although Mrs. Clark encouraged the maintenance and use of the Korean language among Koreans, she also encouraged Korean students to accommodate the white majority. For example, she explained to me that she often advised her students to change their names to "American" ones "to make it easier for them." In her study on Korean American college students, Eun-Young Kim (1993a) found that the majority of Korean students had taken "American names." Kim argues that the use of American names reflects Korean parents' desire for their children to be accepted into American society. Mrs. Clark asserted that changing names was an issue of pragmatism. She felt that it was important to maintain Korean culture but that it was more appropriate for this to be done at home or among fellow Koreans.

In short, Mrs. Clark and other Korean adults encouraged Korean students to adopt a dual identity. They encouraged Korean students to conform to certain American/white, middle-class behaviors in order to succeed in the United States, but they also encouraged Korean students to preserve aspects of the Korean culture. This strategy of a dual identity is similar to the strategy of "accommodation without assimilation," which Gibson (1988, 1991) argues is common among immigrant minorities. Gibson (1988) found that Punjabi parents in California promoted the adoption of "American" values while at school and the maintenance of traditional values at home. Korean-identified students reported similar patterns. In discussing the way in which Korean immigrants view the adoption of American traits, Eun-Young Kim (1993a) writes:

> Korean immigrants trust the United States and believe they can participate in a potentially rewarding mainstream society. They view their dual identity as additive and complementary, not as oppositional and conflicting. Becoming an American does not cause conflict in most Korean immigrants. New elements are selectively added without evoking any sense of loss to a past collective identity. (p. 230)

For Mrs. Clark and the Korean parents, the decision to adopt "American" ways is a pragmatic strategy. They are optimistic that the efforts to become more like "Americans" will be rewarded with success. It is important to note that the Korean parents realize that their children cannot be successful unless they make accommodations to the American culture.

In short, their accommodation is both a recognition of their subordinate status in this country as well as a signal of their belief in social mobility. The success of the Korean students' dual identity is difficult to assess and deserves a separate study. Korean-identified students seemed to believe that they had developed the solution for being Korean in the predominately non-Korean world of Academic. Koreans claimed that their success was marked by their ability to get along with Americans (whites). Brian

Sung said, "I've heard from American kids, even though they can't always tell, they have more respect for Koreans. They think Koreans are better [than other Asians]. Koreans click better [with whites]." Despite Brian's assertions, most non-Asians could not tell the difference between Koreans and other Asian Americans.

The Issue of Gender

Although Korean-identified students viewed their Korean ethnicity as the primary aspect of their identity when dealing with non-Koreans, within the Korean student community they also saw gender as being central to an individual's identity. Korean-identified boys held traditional ideas regarding gender roles. They often made sexist comments regarding how girls and women should behave. Korean-identified girls complained that Korean parents thought boys were better than girls and that this attitude of male superiority persisted among their male peers.

Kay Rowe's relationship with Tom Sun and David Kim illustrates how sexism operates within the Korean-identified student community. Kay, Tom, and David were part of the group of Korean students who frequented the music room. Kay, an eleventh grader, and Tom and David, ninth graders, interacted like siblings. Kay helped them with their homework and advised them about teachers and classes. Although Tom and David clearly liked Kay, they were quick to point out that she was "just a girl." The implicit message was that she was not as important as a boy and that she did not have the same rights as a boy.

On one occasion, Kay wore short pants to school, and she was criticized by Tom and David for being improper. When Kay pointed out that they were also wearing short pants, they responded by saying that it was "okay for boys to wear shorts, but girls should wear dresses or long pants." This remark sparked off a debate that led the boys to make the following comment, "You know, Korean men have a reputation for being real chauvinists. . . . (*laughter*) Korean men think they should beat their wives regularly . . . at least once a day. . . . (*laughter*)." Although Kay and other Korean-identified girls were bothered by this type of behavior, they handled their experiences privately. The issue of sexism was not dealt with openly in the formal Korean-identified student community (e.g., KSA). Additionally, Korean-identified girls did not choose to seek support from outside the Korean community. According to one of my informants, a formal feminist/women's group formed at Academic High the year after I left. Despite the fact that this group was open to all students, the only two students of Asian descent to join the group were Asian American–identified students (a Korean girl and a Vietnamese girl).

Although the issue of how Korean girls deal with their experiences of sexism is beyond the scope of this book, my data on interracial relations suggest that one reason Korean-identified girls did not confront the boys' sexism was that they considered their ethnicity to be more central than their gender to their role as outsiders at Academic High. Some of the Korean-identified girls suggested that the issue of gender relations was a private one that they would handle when they were ready to consider marriage. On one occasion while I was talking with a group of Korean-identified girls, they began to complain about Korean boys, and one of the girls mentioned that she had heard that "Chinese guys were good husbands" and that she planned to marry a Chinese or an American" man. "Good husbands," according to these girls, were men who respected their wives and treated them "nicely." They also noted, however, that their parents wanted them to marry economically successful Korean men.

Different Identities

Although most Korean students at Academic High attempted to forge a dual identity around the strategy of accommodation without assimilation, there were some who rejected the identity prescribed by the Korean community. These students rejected anything associated with their Korean identity in an attempt to be more like the dominant/white group. For these Korean students, the imitating of white behavior evolved into idolizing all that was associated with middle-class white people.

These students turned the hatred and racism that they had experienced on themselves. They made fun of themselves and other Asian Americans, as if to say that they would make fun of themselves before anyone else could. They referred to themselves as "chinks" and to Korean activities as "chink activities." When I asked them why they did this, they laughed and said they thought it was "funny" or "no big deal."

Linda Park was one of these students. Although Linda would sometimes socialize with other Korean students, she preferred to socialize with white students. Like the majority of Korean-identified students, Linda believed that Koreans were superior to other Asians, but she believed that this was true because she and other Koreans were more like whites socially and physically. She made this comment regarding the physical attractiveness of one of her Korean girlfriends, "A lot of people think she's Amerasian, you know half and half, because she's so pretty. She's really Americanized." Linda wanted to be more Americanized (i.e., more like middle-class white people) and less like Koreans. A few days after this conversation, Linda approached me in the lunchroom and said that she thought that Americans (whites) could distinguish between Koreans and other Asians because Koreans look more like whites: "My American friend, Joanne, said that Koreans have better-looking faces than other Asians. . . . You know, more American [white] looking."

Linda's preference for white physical features is reminiscent of the African American children in Clark and Clark's (1947) classic study. Like the African American children in that study, Linda prefers white characteristics over those associated with her own racial group. Linda's attitudes reflect the self-hatred that often comes with attempts to conform to white standards (Phinney, 1989). Sue and Sue (1971) describe Asians who exhibited self-hating characteristics as marginal people. The Sues explain that self-hatred among marginal people is a manifestation of the internal conflict that they experience in their attempt to assimilate into white society. The irony of Linda's self-hatred was revealed when I interviewed Linda's white friend, Joanne. Joanne volunteered that she had a difficult time distinguishing Koreans from other Asians but had told Linda otherwise "because she wanted to hear it."

I also found two Korean students who identified not only as Koreans, but also as Asian Americans. Lee Kim Sun participated in the KSA and sometimes participated in ASA activities as well. She made an unsuccessful bid to become an officer in the KSA during the eleventh-grade year. Unlike her Korean peers, Lee Kim was interested in learning about other Asian cultures. For example, she took Chinese-language classes at the high school next to Academic High. She explained that Koreans were culturally distinct from other Asians but shared common experiences of racism.

Young Hun Pak, quoted earlier, was another student who developed a pan-Asian identity that included her Korean identity. For Young, being Korean concerned her specific cultural heritage. It was about the specific food and language of her home life. Young explained that identifying as Korean only, however, failed to integrate her American experience. Additionally, she explained that identifying solely with her Korean culture would be identifying with a sexist culture that she hated. Finally, Young argued that in the United States the experience of racism bound all Asians together. I talk more about Young in the section on students who exhibit Asian American identifications.

ASIAN-IDENTIFIED STUDENTS

To a certain extent, most of the non-Korean students of Asian descent shared a pan-Asian identity. The first group I discuss called themselves

Asians and included the majority of Asian American students at Academic High. Members of the Asian-identified group were diverse in terms of ethnicity, social class (merchant/middle-class to poor), and English-language skills. Most of them lived in racially integrated neighborhoods on the west side or south side of the city. Most of these students were immigrants from China, Hong Kong, and Taiwan or refugees from Cambodia, Laos, and Vietnam. A few of the American-born Asians belonged to this identity group.

Asian-identified students had one identity based on their pan-ethnic consciousness and one identity that was specific to their ethnic background. Loosely speaking, students would stress their pan-Asian identities in interracial situations and would stress their specific ethnic-group affiliation within Asian circles. Their ability to express both an Asian identity and a specific ethnic identity seems to support Erickson and Shultz's (1982) notion that pan-ethnic identities do not preclude specific ethnic identities.

In general, these students associated solely with other students of Asian descent. They rarely interacted with non-Asians outside of classes. These students noted that they were "most comfortable around other Asians" because they shared similar cultures. Asian-identified students also explained that non-Asians treated all Asians in the same way and that therefore they should stick together for support. As one Asian student explained, "I feel more comfortable with Asians than I do with Americans, and just being with them will relieve the daily pressure from school and outside." Teddy Lee, a Chinese immigrant from Hong Kong, reflected on the differences and similarities among Asians:

> First of all, if you talk about people from Laos, Cambodia, or Vietnam, most of them [have] been through war and a lot of them came as refugees. So there is a similarity; they are all refugees. And for certain Chinese, like for lucky people like me, we never been through any war, we don't have any similarity between them. But, there's only one thing we have in common—that being Asian . . . a lot of us been picked on by other kind of race.

Although Teddy recognized the differences between him and his Southeast Asian friends, he also believed that all Asians receive similar treatment at the hands of non-Asians. He asserted that this common experience of discrimination joined Asians together. Asian-identified students also noted that Asians share difficulties with English. Despite this assertion, these students generally spoke to each other in English.

Living Up to Standards

Of all the Asian Americans at Academic High, Asian-identified students were most like the model minorities described by the media—quiet, respectful of authority, and hardworking. Between classes these students could be found studying, talking about schoolwork, playing chess, or working on computers. The high-achieving, Asian-identified students participated in activities such as the physics club or math club. Many of the average- and lower-achieving Asian students worked as library aides. The quiet and studious behavior of all the Asian-identified students led some of the other Asian American groups to refer to them as the "nerds." Although they had an image as successful students, Asian students experienced varying levels of school achievement. (The issue of student achievement is addressed in the next chapter.)

The Asian-identified students were similar to the immigrant minorities described by Ogbu (1987, 1991). Like Ogbu's immigrant minorities, these Asians believed that hard work would bring them success and that success would bring respect from the dominant group. They believed that the best ways to deal with confrontation were to avoid it or to be silent. Motivated by a desire to honor their families, they spoke about the importance of doing what their parents wanted them to do.

Although these students believed in the value of hard work and education, they also recognized that discrimination would limit their potential. They did not challenge discrimination or speak directly about inequality, but instead they altered their expectations to fit what they perceived to be their opportunities. For example, Thai Le, a high-achieving, Asian-identified student, explained that although he wanted to be a lawyer and a politician, he would become an engineer because he speaks with an Asian accent. He suggested that because of my American-born status and my "good English" that I should become a politician to represent other Asians.

Asian-identified students recognized and accepted that non-Asians cannot distinguish among the different Asian ethnic groups. Rather than fighting this ethnic lumping, Asian-identified students seemed to hope that all Asians would live up to the standards of the model minority stereotype. These students spoke about how important it was for all Asians to work hard, get good grades, and stay out of trouble. Their attitudes contributed to tensions with the Asian new wavers, who were low achievers with antischool attitudes. The Asian-identified students who were most outspoken regarding "living up to standards" were the high achievers. These students saw the new wavers as troublemakers. Thai Le asserted that Asians who failed to work hard were an embarrassment to him and other Asians who tried hard to excel. In his words:

> It hurts me to see some of them not living up . . . to what I . . .
> what my family considers to be the standards. Like we should be
> law-abiding citizens and do our work and not mess around. So,
> if I hear something bad about my group on TV or something, I
> get really hurt because they are messing up our reputation in this
> country. They [non-Asians], unless they are in contact with a lot
> of Asian people, they won't be able to tell the difference between
> Asians.

Thai's statement reflects his deep desire to earn respect from white Americans. It also demonstrates his belief that his respect is tied to other Asians because non-Asians cannot distinguish among Asians. Thai was not alone in this analysis. Hung Chau, another top-ranked student, often made disparaging remarks about new wave Asians. Hung thought that they were lazy and stupid, and he seemed embarrassed by them. Neither Thai or Hung invested much energy into distinguishing among ethnic groups, but instead they seemed to accept that non-Asians grouped all Asians together and therefore treated all Asians the same way.

Language and Identity

Language is often a symbol of identity. Language differences among Asian ethnic groups have been noted to work against a pan-Asian alliance among Asians who do not speak English (Espiritu, 1992). Before entering the field, I assumed that fluency in English would contribute to a pan-Asian identity among the students at Academic High. Similarly, I assumed that limited proficiency in English would limit the formation of a pan-ethnic identity. Although I did find that speaking English positively influenced a pan-Asian alliance, I found that knowledge of multiple languages also promoted pan-ethnicity. For example, when asked about their ethnicity, a number of ethnic Chinese from Cambodia initially told me that they were Cambodian. After some time, they told me that they were actually Chinese and that they were born in Cambodia and that Cambodian was their first language. One student commented that he thought they all felt that they were both Cambodian and Chinese. Another said, "Sometimes you just don't know what to say when you speak a lot of languages."

Interethnic Tensions

While students who identified as Asians expressed a pan-Asian identity, they also expressed strong connections to their specific ethnic groups. Students often argued over the current political situations in their native countries. The following excerpt from my fieldnotes of April 10, 1989, describes an interaction during lunch between Han Tran, a Vietnamese student who hung out with new wave students and Asian-identified students, and three students who were ethnic Chinese from Cambodia and identified themselves as Asians.

> Ming is reading an article in the *New York Times* about the Vietnamese withdrawing troops from Cambodia. Han began to look over Ming's shoulder—
>
> *Han*: I'm insulted that they use the term invader for the Vietcong!
> *Ming*: Well, they are invaders!!
>
> Han began to jump up and down protesting. Name calling and vigorous political debate continues.

Although Han regularly initiated such political arguments with his friends, the disagreements did not permanently upset the social group.

Mei Mei Wong, the vice president of the ASA, was another example of a student who had strong ties to her specific ethnic group and still identified as an Asian. When asked about her ethnicity, Mei Mei responded with, "I'm Taiwanese . . . I'm not Chinese." In fact, whenever people made the mistake of saying that she was Chinese, Mei Mei launched into a political discussion regarding Taiwan's right to independence from China. Despite her devotion to her native country, Mei Mei believed that a pan-Asian alliance in the United States was necessary "to educate people about Asians." Mei Mei asserted that Asians needed to band together because the individual ethnic groups were too small to work alone.

Intra-Asian relations have historically been strained by old national rivalries (Espiritu, 1992; Melendy, 1977). Asian-identified students reported that their parents did not socialize with Asians who were from ethnic groups different from their own because of political differences in their native lands. In contrast to this, political differences did not disturb the Asian-identified students' social groups at Academic High.

Another instance in which Asian-identified students expressed their specific ethnic identities was when I asked about their plans and dreams regarding future romantic relationships. Boys were more adamant than girls about wanting to marry someone from their own ethnic group. Han Tran, the Vietnamese student introduced earlier, explained that although he had Chinese, Cambodian, and Vietnamese friends, that he would only marry a Vietnamese woman. Han explained that he wanted to marry an "old-fashioned Vietnamese woman" because he wanted a wife who would obey him. Similar to the Korean-identified girls, some Asian-identified girls reported being open to marrying an American (white) person. All the

Asian-identified students explained that their parents preferred that they marry a person from their own ethnic group. Some of these students told me that although their parents wanted them to marry someone from the same ethnic group, they would accept marriage to a white person before marriage to any other Asian ethnic. The parents' attitudes toward inter-Asian marriage points to the tension among Asian ethnic groups. Their acceptance of marriage to a white person suggests that they have recognized and accepted the dominance of white people in this country.

Social Class and Identity

As noted earlier, students who identified as Asian represented a range of social-class backgrounds. Unlike the Korean-identified students, the Asian-identified students did not view social class as being central to their identities. The exception to this were the Taiwanese students who were from middle-class and merchant families. Although the Taiwanese students identified as Asian and had friends who were from a variety of class backgrounds, they were critical of Asian families whom they perceived to be poor. On one occasion, Mei Jen Lee, a Taiwanese student who identified as Asian and Taiwanese, and Ming, an ethnic Chinese student from Cambodia who identified as Asian and Chinese, were eating lunch and talking about the high cost of college tuition. When Ming mentioned that his family was on public assistance, Mei Jen expressed her shock and disgust. Later she commented to me that she could not understand how anyone could accept public assistance. The following is an excerpt from an essay written by a Taiwanese student:

> People tend to categorize me into a false stereotype just by looking at [my] face. Oh, how much I want to break away from them all and convince the world that I am not like "them." But how can I? When there are children running around dirty, barefoot, and ill dressed? Children living in run-down houses who look like me. Surely you must think that I hate my black hair and almond shaped eyes. I despise only those who do not try to better themselves. When I saw them, I asked myself, "why do they look like that?"

This student recognized that, although she saw herself as being different from low-income Asians, non-Asians saw all Asians as being the same. She was embarrassed by and for these low-income Asians. Later in the essay she wrote that she wanted to understand the experiences of the low-income Asian children and to help them. My Taiwanese American informants told me that they sympathized with the attitudes held by the Korean-identified students and understood why they wanted a separate group. They reported that they could not form a group for Taiwanese American students because there were not enough of them at the school. Overlooking the social-class differences among Asians and stressing the similarities, they chose to identify with the other Asians. In short, Asian-identified students looked beyond social-class, ethnic, and other differences in order to forge a pan-ethnic identity.

NEW WAVERS: A CULTURE OF RESISTANCE

Most new wave students were ethnic Chinese, Vietnamese, or Cambodian. Most came to the United States in the second and third waves of refugee arrival. Although most new wavers were from working-class and poor families, there were new wavers who were the children of merchants. Like the students who identified as Asian, the new wavers had a pan-ethnic identity. They expressed a pan-ethnic identity among non-Asians and expressed their specific ethnic identity among other Asian Americans.

Unlike the other Asian American students at Academic High and unlike the "typical" immigrant described by cultural ecologists (Ogbu, 1987, 1991), the new wavers did not see education as the key to success in the United States. In fact, new wavers made it their business to get around school rules and schoolwork. New wave students could be found hanging around on the school's southeast lawn smoking, talking, and listening to music throughout the school day. While students who identified as Korean or Asian spoke about family obligation, new wavers were more concerned with what their peers thought. New wave students complained that their parents were "old fashioned" and did not understand them. For these peer-oriented students, the most important thing was social acceptance from their new wave peers. These students were the antithesis of the Asian model minority.

Negotiating Entrance into the New Wave Community

Initially I found it difficult to gain access to the new wave students. Although they were not openly hostile to outsiders, they were generally suspicious. My outsider status was marked by my clothes, my adult age, my role as a researcher, and the fact that I am American-born. From the outside, the new wave students seemed to be a tight-knit group. They dressed alike, ate lunch together, sat together at Asian Students' Association meetings, and socialized together before and after school.

During my first few interviews with new wave students, I discovered that new wave students seldom referred to themselves as new wave, at least not to outsiders. Despite the fact that these students dressed like new wave students, socialized exclusively with other new wave students, and were identified by non–new wave Asian Americans as being new wave, these students always responded negatively when asked whether or not they were new wave. I learned why these students did not identify themselves as new wavers to outsiders during the first formal interview I conducted with a new wave girl. Lan Quan, an ethnic Chinese from Vietnam, was introduced to me by an Asian American–identified informant who described Lan as a new waver. After waiting months to interview a new wave student I was overenthusiastic when I met Lan. Instead of following my regular set of guiding questions, I launched right into questions about her new wave status.

> *SL*: Are you new wave?
> *Lan*: No.
> *SL*: Do other people think you are new wave?
> *Lan*: Yes, they think I dress so nice and cool, but I don't.
> *SL*: What are new wave students like?
> *Lan*: Some is nice, some not. Some, they drink, smoke, and go to
> party every night. I don't drink or smoke.

As soon as I asked Lan whether she was a new waver, she became very tense and defensive. It was obvious that I had offended her. Later in the interview, Lan asserted that she was new wave but, "one of the nice one[s]." Apparently, Lan did not want non–new wave people to consider her to be new wave because other Asians had negative images of new wave students. Han Tran, the Vietnamese student introduced earlier, confirmed my suspicion that new wave students were looked down on by other Asians. In his words, "There's a problem with other people; they think since you're new wave that you're all bad."

After my interview with Lan, I learned to be more careful about how I approached new wave students. Later I heard from other students that Lan had warned her new wave girlfriends that I could not be trusted. I did not gain real acceptance from new wave students until I met Lee Chau. I met Lee, an ethnic Chinese from Vietnam, at an ASA bake sale. Lee sat at the ASA bake sale for three class periods in a row. Although he did not work at the bake sale, he used it as an excuse to miss his classes. We chatted informally about his ideas about Academic High and about my research. Personable from the beginning, Lee invited me to a party at a local dance club that weekend. Although I did not attend the party, Lee agreed to show me life on the southeast lawn.

As an informant, Lee proved to be rather colorful. Since he was often truant, it was difficult to schedule appointments with him. However, because he held high status on the southeast lawn, his acceptance of me proved to be helpful in my efforts to gain the trust of his buddies. Lee was popular among his male and female peers. An athlete, Lee was well built and, according to his friends, "able to handle himself." In his own words, "I'm not a wimp. I can defend myself. A lot of Asians can't fight, so they have to go around in gangs. They're small. You know Asian guys." During his junior year at Academic High, Lee and another Asian American male were the victims of a racially motivated attack, which took place at a subway station near school. Although Lee was able to get away with minor injuries, this incident confirmed his belief that he had to be able to protect himself.

As a car owner, Lee earned extra status. During the spring, his car stereo provided music for the group on the southeast lawn. In addition to musical entertainment, cars provided students with a means of escape. This is what Lee told me when I asked him about what he did when he cut class,

> You know, we hang on the southeast lawn. Sometimes, if enough cars are available, we go places. Last year a lot of Asians owned cars, and we used to drive to Atlantic City to shoot pool. If we go, you could come with us. Sometimes we just go to the mall and eat.

On the day that I tailed Lee, we spent most of the day on the southeast lawn, where he smoked, listened to music, played volleyball, and talked.

The Significance of Style: "New Wavers Wear Black"

Much has been written about the significance of clothing style as a social marker (Eckert, 1989; Hebdige, 1979). Because clothing is always worn in public, it serves as an important symbol of group membership to members and nonmembers (Eckert, 1989). Hebdige (1979) argued that all social groups, even those who appear to be "normal," send messages with their clothing. In writing about the significance of the conventional clothing style worn by "average" people, Hebdige said: "Ultimately, if nothing else, they are expressive of 'normality' as opposed to 'deviance' (i.e., they are distinguished by their relative invisibility, their appropriateness, their 'naturalness')" (p. 101). Both Asian- and Asian American–identified students chose clothes that *were* within the "normal" range, although some of the students from higher social-class backgrounds often wore slightly more expensive clothes. In contrast, Korean students chose clothes that advertised their middle-class status and their future yuppie status.

Of all the Asian American students, however, the new wavers exhibited the most flamboyant style. From my first day at Academic, I heard about the "new wave kids." Their Asian American peers described new wavers as the Asians who "wear black clothes," "spike up their hair," and "like to party." The new wave students were named after the new-wave style music that many of them liked. Their style separated them from all the other Asian American students and made them easy to identify. Hebdige (1979) has argued that the communication of difference is the purpose of the clothing styles chosen by subcultures: "The communication of a significant difference, then (and the parallel communication of group identity), is the 'point' behind the style of all spectacular subcultures" (p. 102).

New wave boys wore loose-fitting shirts and loose-fitting black trousers, which new wavers told me "looked cool when you dance." They used hair gel to spike their hair up. The girls wore tight black jeans and black or white tops, Most of the girls wore their hair long and used gel in their hair to spike their bangs. In contrast to Asian-, Korean-, and Asian American–identified girls, the new wave girls wore a lot of makeup. New wavers told me that they chose their clothes to look "cool." They were acutely aware of the Asian nerd image, and their clothes were chosen to deflect that image. Many new wavers considered the wearing of new wave clothes to be the first step to becoming new wave. Although new wavers had a reputation for always wearing black, the most socially prominent new wavers sometimes strayed from their black uniforms by wearing jeans.

While the new wavers rejected the nerd image of Asians, they did not reject all things Asian. Many of the new wave boys wore pieces of Asian jewelry, such as 24-karat gold chain necklaces and pieces of jade. During the time I was doing fieldwork, I was in the habit of wearing a jade ring and a jade pendant. The ring caught the attention of my male new wave informants, and after they got to know me better, they began to quiz me on my understanding of the significance of jade. They asked me questions like, "Do you know what jade means?" or "Where did you get that?" or "Why do you always wear that jade ring?" When I told them that my grandmother taught me that jade was good luck and protected the wearer, my new wave friends seemed pleased. One new wave informant told me that they asked me these questions to determine if I were really Asian. Their testing of me suggests that culture is significant in intra-Asian situations.

Interethnic Relations Among New Wavers

To outsiders the new wavers seemed like a cohesive group without internal differences, but once I began spending more time with the new wave students, I heard some interesting comments regarding intergroup relations and specifically regarding ethnicity. Although the new wave Asians were a pan-Asian group, they were sensitive to ethnic differences.

Students regularly referred to each other's ethnic backgrounds in the form of teasing (e.g., "You Chinese are all the same"). I noted that arguments about everything from sports to dating often resulted in the exchange of such slurs as, "You Vietcong scum." As with the Asian-identified students, ethnic slurs and national competition, however, did not seem to disturb the pan-Asian composition of Academic's new wave students.

Although new wavers socialized primarily with other new wavers, new wave students and Asian-identified students saw each other as Asians. A few of the more marginal new wavers (e.g., Han Tran) socialized with new wave students and with lower-achieving, Asian-identified students. The Asian-identified students who expressed direct hostility toward the new wavers were high-achieving, Asian-identified students like Thai Le (who was introduced earlier). Mun Chau, another high-achieving, Asian-identified student, blamed new wavers for threatening the reputation of Asians. Mun refused to join the ASA because there were new wavers in the group. According to his friends, Mun's brother had been a top student until he became involved with a group of new wavers.

Neighborhood New Wavers

While Asian- and Asian American–identified students socialized primarily with other Academic High students, new wavers reported that many of their friends went to other schools. The new wave students at Academic High were on the margin of a larger group of Asian American adolescents who were alienated from school. In her research on Southeast Asian refugee adolescents, Peters (1988) identified a group of "problem youth" who have either dropped out of school or were at risk for dropping out and who engaged in "antisocial" behavior. Like the "problem youth" in Peters's study, the new wave students' friends engaged in resistant behavior. The new wave students at Academic High argued that their friends were the "real new wavers," those who drank, gambled, carried weapons, and belonged to gangs. Academic High new wavers reported that they hung out at some of the same clubs and wore the same clothes as the "real new wavers" but did not participate in the violence. They also reported that the "real new wavers" assumed that they were smart because they went to Academic High. They learned about the harsh realities of interracial tension and police brutality from friends who were "real new wavers."

New Wavers and Gender Relations

New wavers attempted to present an image of themselves as sexually mature and active. New wavers spoke about sex and engaged in heterosexual flirtations and dating. By contrast, Korean-, Asian-, and Asian American–identified students rarely spoke about sex or sexuality. New wave boys considered themselves to be superior to other Asian American boys in areas of sexuality. In his study on white working-class boys, Willis (1977) found similar attitudes among members of the counterculture toward the boys who conformed to school rules. In addition to presenting an image of sexuality, new wave boys also tried to present an image of physical toughness. For new wave boys, presenting a stereotypically Western image of masculinity was part of their attempt to debunk the nerd image of Asian men. Asian American scholars and writers have asserted that the stereotype of Asians as quiet model minorities has framed Asian men as feminine and passive (Cheung, 1990, 1993). Cheung (1993) wrote, "precisely because quietness is associated with the feminine, as is the 'East' in relation to the 'West' (in Orientalist discourse), Asian and Asian American men too have been 'feminized' in American popular culture" (p. 2).

Compared to other Asian American girls, new wave girls spent a lot of time flirting with boys. As noted earlier, new wave girls wore more makeup than their non–new wave peers. While Asian- and Korean-identified girls wore conservative clothing, new wave girls wore clothes that exposed more of their bodies (e.g., low-cut blouses). For new wave girls, presenting a more sexually mature image was one way they resisted authority and the "good girl" image promoted by the schools and by their parents. Sexuality as a form of resistance has been observed among white working-class girls as well (McLaren, 1982; McRobbie, 1978).

Although the new wave boys and girls both presented sexual images of themselves, new wave boys held a double standard regarding sex and sexuality. For example, new wave boys admired other new wave boys who were sexually experienced with girls, but they looked down on new wave girls who were sexually active. In fact, new wave boys did not even believe that "good girls" should talk about sex. One new wave boy complained that all new wave girls were "fast." In his words, "One thing is unmentionable. . . new wave girls are very, they're infatuated. The fastest girl, the longest relationship she had was two days." New wave boys wanted their girlfriends to be sexually inexperienced, and new wave girls who broke these rules were labeled "bad" or "fast." Although new wave boys labeled girls who spoke about sex as "bad," they flirted with these same girls. Dorothy Chin, the president of the ASA and one of the most popular new wave students at Academic High, was criticized by new wave males for being too fast. In her presence, the new wave males were nice to Dorothy; they joked around with her and asked for her opinions. Behind her back, however, some of these same boys criticized Dorothy for talking openly about sex. Han said that while he liked Dorothy, she "talked about stuff girls [are] not supposed to talk about." Han asserted that he would not marry someone like Dorothy. For her part, Dorothy seemed unaware of the boys' double standards. She reported that she was equally comfortable with males and females.

Reasons for Group Solidarity

The pan-Asian identity among new wave students was influenced by their relationships with and attitudes toward non-Asians. Like students who identified as Asian, new wave students simply explained that they "feel more comfortable with Asians." Some explained that their "comfort" with Asians was based on language or culture. These students complained that they were embarrassed by their "broken English" and that non-Asians often ridiculed their English. Other new wave Asians emphasized that their "comfort" with other Asians grew out of their discomfort with non-Asians.

New wavers spoke of being stereotyped and being grouped together with all other Asians. Lan complained that "they [non-Asians] all consider us chink—one thing. They can't identify and separate us." Experience had shown new wave students that the inability of non-Asians to distinguish among the different Asian groups has meant that Asians receive equal discrimination. Han Tran described his experience with some bitterness: "They specify us as all Asian. Some time when a Cambodian get in trouble with them, they start call us all names." Like the Asian-identified students, the new wavers have developed their pan-ethnic identification in response to common experiences with discrimination.

As a group, the new wave students had few friendships with non-Asians. Although there were non-Asian students who sported a new wave style, the Asian new wave students and these non-Asian new wave students had no contact. In interviews and conversations with these students, they all spoke about problems with discrimination and name calling. Although they recognized that they had problems with whites and African Americans, their harshest complaints were directed at African Americans. This topic is discussed further in Chapter 5.

The relationships that new wave Asians had with Korean-identified students also helped to solidify the new wave student group. Korean-identified students found new wave students to be among the most offensive of the Asians. They mocked the clothing that new wave students wore. One Korean-identified student ridiculed new wave students for failing to be like Americans. In his words, "They [new wave] try to be so American, but they fail so bad. They just look stupid." Korean-identified students were not critical of the new wavers because they were trying to be like Americans, but because they were imitating what the Korean-identified students thought were the "wrong Americans." New wavers were buying clothes at stores where working-class African Americans and working-class whites shopped. By contrast, Korean-identified students emulated white middle- and upper-middle-class students and looked down on what they saw as the working-class style of the new wavers. According to the Korean-identified students' standards, "good" Americans are white and middle-class, and "bad" Americans are working-class whites and all African Americans. The new wave students were aware that the Koreans looked down on non-Korean Asians, and they often complained that Koreans were "snobby." Thanh, a new wave male, described the difference between Korean-identified students and other Asian Americans: "Most of the time I see Koreans think they're somebody. You see the Chinese, Vietnamese, Cambodian, Laos, or whatever—we're all friends, but the Koreans act like they don't know us."

As noted earlier, high-achieving, Asian-identified students criticized new wave students for giving Asians a bad name. New wavers were aware of this condemnation and justified their own behavior by asserting that the high-achieving, Asian-identified students worked too hard and were missing out on all the fun.

Thus the new wave-identified students formed their identities in reaction to negative experiences with the high-achieving, Asian-identified students, the Korean-identified students, and the non-Asian students.

ASIAN AMERICAN-IDENTIFIED STUDENTS

Finally, there was a small group of Asian American students who identified themselves as Asian Americans. This group included students from a range of ethnic groups (Korean, Chinese, Vietnamese) and a range of social-class backgrounds (merchant/middle-class to working-class). Most had been in the United States since they were young children, a few had come in the last five years, and a few were American-born. Like the high-achieving, Asian-identified students, Asian American–identified students were generally strong academic students. Many of the high-achieving, Asian-identified students and the Asian American–identified students regularly ate lunch together and engaged in debates over political and social issues. Like the new wavers and the Asian group, Asian American–identified students felt that they had the most in common with other Asian Americans. Unlike the Asian and the new wave students, the Asian American–identified students argued that racism should be confronted directly.

Although the Asians and the new wavers all spoke about experiences with discrimination, neither group felt empowered to challenge or question the status of the dominant group. Instead, some of them internalized the racism they experienced and referred to themselves as "chinks." On the other hand, students who identified as Asian Americans felt empowered to speak out against racism. They argued that all Asian Americans should work together to fight racism, and they saw white people as the primary holders of institutional power and the beneficiaries of racism. Sherry Wong, an Asian American–identified student of Chinese descent, put it like this:

> I just feel that like since we get pushed around because we are in the minority in this giant United States. And we get pushed around a lot and we should help each other out when there is a problem. And not just look at another person and say "oh that's not part of my business" and just go away.

The most progressive Asian American–identified students also advocated building bridges with other people of color. This issue is discussed further in Chapter 6.

Like the politics of Asian American activists during the 1960s, the politics of the Asian American–identified students were confrontational (Espiritu, 1992; Omi & Winant, 1986). These students resisted behavior that they believed accommodates the dominant group. For example, Young Hun Pak, the Korean student introduced earlier who identified as Asian American, criticized the KSA for throwing an annual KSA luncheon for the faculty in order to "get acceptance." At the luncheon, KSA members dressed up in traditional Korean clothes and served "Americanized" Korean food to the faculty free of charge. Young asserted that the Luncheon played into stereotypes that Asians were exotic and subservient. Another way that Asian Americans fought racism was by speaking out against the model minority stereotype. Xuan Nguyen complained that "they [non-Asians] don't think about the negative impact the model minority myth would have. They don't think about all the dropouts because they are too busy talking about all the success stories." According to these students, the model minority stereotype hides the reality of the many Asian students who are not successful. Asian American–identified students and the high-achieving, Asian-identified students often argued over the accuracy of the model minority stereotype and the impact of the stereotype on people of Asian descent. Asian-identified students argued that Asians should be proud of the stereotype and work hard to live up to the model minority standards, while Asian American–identified students argued that the stereotype was essentially racist.

"We're Asian Americans, Not Orientals"

Asian American–identified students were adamant about being called Asian American and not Oriental. Like Asian American activists beginning in the late 1960s and the early 1970s, the Asian American–identified students rejected the term *Oriental* because it connotes images of the passive, the exotic, and the foreign. By contrast, Asian and new wave students would occasionally use the term to describe themselves and never argued when people referred to them as Oriental. It must be noted, however, that the terms *Oriental* and *Asian American* both express pan-Asian identities but have different ideological outlooks (Espiritu, 1992). Whether or not the term *Oriental* should be used to describe people from Asian backgrounds was a point of contention between Asian American–identified students and all other Asian students. Asian American students argued that the term was degrading and should never be used. Asian-, new wave–, and Korean-identified students argued that it was ridiculous to get upset over labels.

American, Too

A significant factor that distinguished students who identified as Asian American from those who identified as Asian or new wave was that Asian Americans saw themselves as being American as well as Asian. For them, being Asian American meant forging a new identity based on their Asian and American identities. In Xuan's words:

> I have experiences that are similar to other Asians that live in America. That my culture is not all Asian and it's not all American. It's something entirely different. And it's not like some people say, that it's a mixture. It's like another whole different thing. When I say I'm Asian American I feel like I establish a root for myself here. My parents think of themselves as Vietnamese because their roots are in Vietnam. Being Asian American is like a way to feel like I belong.

By establishing "roots" for herself, Xuan gave herself a sense of entitlement. She no longer saw herself as a visitor who must adapt to the host's demands or depend on her host's goodwill. I would argue that Xuan's identification as an American gave her the sense of empowerment that she needed to challenge racism.

By comparison, students who identified as Korean, Asian, or new wave did not see themselves as American. These students referred to all nonwhite people by their race and referred to white people as Americans.

When I asked Korean-, Asian-, and new wave–identified students to describe a "typical" American, they described a blond, blue-eyed person. They saw themselves as the "other" and saw whites as the norm. According to these students, only white people were "real" Americans. Additionally, I noted that most Korean-, Asian-, and new wave–identified students did not think of me as an American despite the fact that they knew that I was American-born.

A brief description of Xuan's immigration history points to a possible connection between the length of time in the United States and attitudes toward the United States. Born in Vietnam, Xuan came to the United States in 1975 when she was two years of age. Because Xuan came to the United States at such a young age, she was very comfortable with the culture of non-Asians. In fact, she was more comfortable with the English language than with Vietnamese. Xuan noted that she had always been able to get along with her non-Asian peers at school. Despite these facts, non-Asians who did not know her often assumed that Xuan could not speak English. Although Xuan saw herself as being Asian and American, she pointed out that non-Asians continued to see her as a foreigner. Xuan asserted that all Asians suffer from this assumption. In her words:

> It's like this when you come to America, people don't know the difference between a 1975 refugee and like a third-generation Japanese American. So, whatever you do, they'll look at you the same. So, in my feeling, it's like we all share the same history because we're all Asian.

Xuan's experience taught her that regardless of the length of time spent in the United States, Asian Americans cannot escape stereotyping or racism.

The Significance of Names

As noted earlier, some Korean-identified students changed their names to Western ones as a way to ease their experiences in the United States. Some Asian- and new wave–identified students also changed their names to Western ones for similar reasons. One new wave student who was in the process of choosing an "American name" explained that he was simply tired of having people make fun of his name. In his words, "People make rhymes like 'fee fi fo fum.' I hate it." Culturally insensitive comments like this were reported by students in all of the identity groups, and they told me that there were also teachers who ridiculed them for having "funny names." When Korean-, new wave–, and Asian-identified students took new names, they were trying to protect themselves from further ridicule. Unfortunately, self-protection equaled the silencing of their culture and the silencing of their identities.

Asian American–identified students expressed pride in their ethnic names. Although these students reported that non-Asians often made jokes about their names, they resisted any suggestion that they should change their names to Western ones. Asian American–identified students asserted that people who made jokes about names were "ignorant and stupid." They responded to ridicule by placing the responsibility for change back on the name callers rather than absorbing the ridicule. As Xuan said, "I like my name."

Sexism and Racism

Although there were male and female students who defined themselves as Asian American, two of the most outspoken Asian American–identified students were girls. Xuan and Young saw racism and sexism as being central to their experiences. They explained that as Asian American girls they face racism from non-Asians (male and female) and sexism from men (Asian and non-Asian). Although Korean-, Asian-, and new wave–identified girls all complained about gender inequality, they did not challenge the sexism directly. Asian American–identified girls viewed sexism as something to confront much the way they confront racism.

An example of the way that sexism operated within the Asian American student community occurred one day during lunch when a group of Asian-identified boys drew nipples on two helium balloons and let them loose in the cafeteria. As the balloons flew through the air, the boys mocked the Asian-identified and Asian American–identified girls who tried to pull the balloons down from the ceiling. Although the Asian-identified girls were upset by this incident, they wrote it off to "boys will be boys." Asian American–identified girls were angered by the incident and refused to laugh it off.

Many of the new wave– and Asian-identified boys tried to silence Xuan and the other Asian American–identified girls' charges of sexism. First, they criticized Xuan for being "too loud for a girl" and for "sounding like a guy." Second, they accused Xuan of taking things too seriously and not having a sense of humor. Finally, the boys accused Xuan of being "un-Asian" and "too American." In their eyes, traditional Asian women are supposed to be quiet and passive. Similarly, during the 1960s Asian American women who challenged sexism within the Asian American activist movement were charged with being assimilationist (Lowe, 1991).

On one occasion I overheard an Asian-identified boy suggest that Xuan and Young acted like lesbians. The boy who made the statement and his friends immediately burst into laughter. The purpose of this homophobic baiting was to negatively sanction Xuan and Young's outspoken behavior. In writing about the relationship between sexism and homophobia, Friend (1993) asserts that:

> Girls who are "too independent" not only violate traditional gender role expectations, but are also negatively stigmatized as homosexual. In this way a homophobic label is used to enforce a sexist arrangement and functions to try to keep all students, heterosexual and homosexual alike, from violating what is expected of them in terms of gender role behaviors. (p. 232)

According to the Asian- and new wave–identified boys, Xuan and Young had overstepped the gender line and needed to be put back in their place.

In the following statement, Xuan described her experience with Asian American boys who hold traditional views of women: "They aren't comfortable around me because I'm too outspoken. So they get like, 'Why can't you be like a normal girl? You're not supposed to do this.' I think I make them nervous." Despite the reactions of these boys, Asian American–identified girls confronted boys they thought were being sexist. They celebrated being Asian American women by reading literature written by Asian American women. Xuan suggested that being American has allowed her the freedom to challenge sexist notions in Asian culture. In her words, "If I were Asian, I wouldn't support feminist things, but as an Asian American I can." Xuan believed that in a traditional Asian world there would not be any room for her. Here, Xuan used the term *American* in a positive sense to represent freedom, choice, and possibility. Xuan believed that the term *Asian American* forged her identities as an Asian, as an American, and as a girl together. The year after I left Academic High, a small group of girls formed a feminist union at Academic High. Xuan and Young were the only two girls of Asian American descent who joined the club.

The experiences of the Asian American–identified girls and the Asian American feminists of the 1960s force us to consider who has the authority to define being Asian or Asian American. By asserting that Xuan was not acting "Asian," the Asian- and new wave–identified boys were claiming authority over the definition of "Asian." These boys were claiming what Cornel West (1992) has referred to as racial authenticity. He argues that calls for racial authenticity among certain groups of African Americans are excuses to perpetuate sexism within the African American community. The Asian and new wave boys were similarly trying to silence Asian American girls by calling into question their "Asianness" and their loyalty to other Asian Americans.

Sexual Orientation and Identity

The experience of Stephen Chau illustrates the influence of sexual orientation on ethnic and racial identity. Early in my research, Stephen explained to me that he identified as both an Asian and as a gay male. He belonged to an organization outside of school for gay Asian men. Although he participated in the gay community in the city, he chose to keep his sexual orientation a secret from his Asian-identified peers because he feared their rejection. His efforts to hide his sexuality led him to attend the junior prom with a girl from his neighborhood. His ability to hide his sexual orientation points to the relative invisibility of sexual orientation. Stephen understood that his race made him a visible outsider in a school and in a society dominated by non-Asians. The invisibility of his sexual orientation stood in stark contrast to the visibility of his race/Asianness (Takagi, 1994). Stephen believed that he needed the support of his Asian peers to handle the discrimination he faced based on race. Thus he felt compelled to hide one of his identities in order to protect his membership in another group. His efforts to hide his sexual orientation came at a cost. Stephen often talked about being lonely, and I often found him alone. It should be noted that many Korean-, new wave–, and Asian-identified boys expressed vehement homophobia. These young men also expressed overt sexism. According to their standards, accusing a boy of being effeminate and acting like a "faggot" was the worst possible sanction. Their verbal assaults silenced Stephen, straight girls, and countless gay and lesbian students.

During his senior year in high school, Stephen became friends with a few Asian American–identified students. Eventually he came out to these students and found a social home for himself. He also began to identify himself as Asian American rather than Asian.

The Impact of the Asian American Activist Community

The most active and vocal Asian American–identified students were involved with Asian American issues outside the school. These students wanted to fight inequality and to work to improve conditions for Asian American communities. Several of these students had participated in a summer program sponsored by a progressive Asian American community organization called Asian Americans United (AAU). AAU, founded by a group of Asian Americans who had been active in progressive politics since the late 1960s and early 1970s, fights for educational equity, fair housing, and health care for Asian Americans. AAU has fought against anti-Asian violence and attempted to build bridges with other people of color.

Xuan reported that she began to think of herself as an Asian American after her work with AAU. She also asserted that her work with AAU helped her to stop thinking of herself and other Asian Americans as mere victims. The following is an excerpt from an essay written by an Asian American–identified student who worked as a tutor in the summer program sponsored by AAU:

> Last summer, this particular myth was shattered when we worked in tutorial program with a group of second wave [after 1975] Southeast Asian children. The program was initiated by Asian Americans United. These children were not the "successful" Asians who are able to overcome every obstacle. Their everyday obstacle is survival. During the day, many were left without adult supervision. Many of their parents were out working on farms picking blueberries for $2.25 crate. When we visited them, we found them playing in the dirt and glass that surrounded their homes. One of the buildings, once as majestic as its name, King's Court, is a slum tenement. Two years ago it was condemned as being "unfit for human habitation" by the city's Department of Licenses and Inspections.

According to this student, her experiences working with AAU forced her to see beyond her own experiences and beyond the model minority stereotype.

Although I was a member of AAU before, during, and after my fieldwork at Academic High, I did not know my Asian American–identified informants prior to my research. My connections with AAU, however, did allow me to observe Asian American–identified students outside of school and to continue fieldwork with them after my fieldwork at Academic High ended.

Similar to the Asian-identified and Korean-identified students, the Asian American–identified students looked to adults as role models. For the Asian Americans, however, the adult role models were not their parents, but members of AAU. Although these students obeyed their parents' rules and tried to please them, they often disagreed with their parents about social and political issues. Asian American–identified students' politics were informed by the politics of AAU. Like the adult members of AAU, Asian American–identified students believed that issues of race, class, gender, and sexuality were linked. On the other hand, their parents were strong opponents of communism and were therefore suspicious of any leftist or progressive social/political movements. The Asian American–identified students walked a fine line between following their parents' orders and following their political ideas.

"WE ARE ALL ASIANS":
ASIANS, NEW WAVERS, AND ASIAN AMERICANS

Although students with Asian racial identities divided themselves into three distinct groups, they all recognized one another as Asians. A common way students expressed their pan-Asian identity was through membership in the Asian Students' Association. ASA members were diverse in terms of self-defined identities, ethnicity, social and economic status, length of time in the United States, academic achievement, personal interests, and politics. At the beginning of the school year, the ASA attracted close to a hundred students to the meetings. Most of these students said they attended early meetings because they "wanted to check it out" or they "wanted to see who the other Asians were." ASA members told me that they went to meetings for the social support. One student put it succinctly by saying, "When you go to ASA meetings, you know you're not alone."

Because of differences in personal interests and political outlooks, it was difficult to sustain everyone's interest in the club. After the beginning of the year, the attendance at meetings averaged around 25 members. During most of these meetings, members argued over their different visions of the ASA. ASA officers complained that members were "never happy." New wave members wanted the club to concentrate on sponsoring Asian dances and parties, Asian members wanted the club to sponsor educational/cultural events, and Asian American students thought the club should be more political and educational. Thus participation in the club varied depending on the specific activities. ASA dances and parties often attracted as many as a hundred students. On the other hand, participation on the ASA magazine or at an ASA-sponsored workshop on Asian American history averaged about 12 students. Despite personal and political differences, the members never spoke about dividing the ASA. They seemed to think that one ASA made them "stronger." As one member put it, "we need for us to be united and not go in different directions if we want things to be done . . . . Like educate at least the people in this building about Asians."

One of the most significant displays of pan-Asian identification occurred at the 1989 senior prom, when Asians representing the new wave and Asian groups sat together. Asian American–identified students did not attend the junior or senior proms. The president of the ASA reserved three tables for the ASA. The students at these tables were members of the ASA only in the loosest manner, but they were all Asian. Another striking example of pan-Asian identification was the "Asian graduation party." A few of the new wave students rented a church hall, hired a disc jockey, and invited their Asian friends. When I arrived at the party, I was surprised to find almost 200 Asian students. Although many of the students were from Academic High, there were also students from other schools in the city. Members of the new wave, Asian, and Asian American identity groups were present. In terms of ethnicity, there were Chinese, Vietnamese, Cambodian, and Lao students. The only Korean student I spotted was a student who identified as Asian American. As if to answer my unasked question, an Asian American male said this: "It's a typical Asian party. Everyone who is Asian comes. People hear by word of mouth."

In short, with the exception of students who identified solely as Koreans, Asian American students at Academic High forged a pan-Asian identification as a response to the social conditions in the United States generally and at Academic specifically. Teddy Lee, a Chinese immigrant from Hong Kong, summarized the situation in the following sentence: "Once we come to this country, we [are] all Asian."

CHAPTER 3

Academic Achievement Among Asian Americans

April 4, 1989—Class rankings and SAT scores were the topics of the day. I spent fifth-period lunch listening to Huy, Thai, Xuan, and other high-achieving students talk about the class rankings. Thai was happy that he made it into the top ten. It seems that six of the students in the top ten of the junior class are Asian Americans. Students are already referring to the class of 1990 as the "Asian class." After school I ran into Ming and Chu. Before I ran into them I'd almost forgotten that not all of my informants were high-achieving model minorities. Seeing Ming and Chu reminded me of the low-achieving Asian American students who are silenced by the model minority stereotype.

The model minority stereotype depicts Asian Americans as academic superstars. Images of Asian American math geniuses, computer science experts, and high school valedictorians are ingrained in the minds of Americans. According to the stereotype, Asian Americans are successful in school because they work hard and come from cultures that believe in the value of education. Although, as pointed out in Chapter 1, the popular press has perpetuated the image of the Asian American whiz kid among the general population, scholars have also contributed to the stereotyping of Asian Americans. Most of the scholarly literature on Asian American students focuses on trying to explain the above-average success rates of Asian American students.

EXPLANATIONS FOR ASIAN AMERICAN EDUCATIONAL ACHIEVEMENT

The Cultural Explanation

The most common explanation given for Asian American school success is that Asian cultures promote the value of education. According to this argument, Asian Americans are successful because they are taught to value education and learning. This explanation has been advocated by scholars and by journalists. The cultural explanation was also the most common explanation given by teachers at Academic High to explain high achievement among their Asian American students.

Caudill and De Vos (1956) were among the first to argue for the cultural explanation. Based on their research on Japanese Americans who had settled in Chicago, they conclude that Japanese Americans gain relative success because they exhibit cultural characteristics valued by the dominant group. In a similar vein, Kitano (1969) argues that the "functional compatibility" between Japanese culture and American culture makes it easy for Japanese Americans to adapt to American society. According to these theories, Japanese Americans succeed because their culture matches American culture. More recently, Caplan, Choy, and Whitmore (1991) argue that Southeast Asian refugees are gaining success in the United States because their cultures share features in common with middle-class American culture. In their words, "the emphasis on education and achievement through hard work and the willingness to delay immediate satisfaction for future gains are at the heart of the belief system one associates with the American dream" (p. 130).

Others who have postulated a cultural explanation point to the unique characteristics associated with Asian cultures. These theorists compare Asian cultures with "American" culture and conclude that Asian cultures are more conducive to academic achievement. These authors point to the family-centered nature of Asian families as the single most significant reason for Asian success (Hsu, 1971; Mordkowitz & Ginsberg, 1987; Sung, 1987). They argue that Asian parents teach their children to work hard in school in order to uphold the family honor. Furthermore, they argue that Asian children work hard to please their parents and to avoid the shame and guilt associated with failure. While most theorists writing from this perspective suggest that the desire to please parents contributes to Asian American student success, Pang (1990) cautions that this desire to please can also lead to anxiety among Asian American students.

Although the cultural explanation offers insight into the relationship between home life and student achievement, it is severely limited. First, the cultural explanation fails to account for within-group differences in achievement. The cultural theory explains high achievement, but it does not explain low achievement. Why do some Asian Americans do poorly in school? Another problem with the cultural explanation is that it fails to account for low achievement among Asians in their native countries, where presumably their culture is strongest (Siu, 1992). Furthermore, studies of particular Asian ethnic groups in different countries suggest that school success is not simply a cultural issue. For example, while Korean students in Japan show consistently low achievement, Korean students in the United States demonstrate relatively high academic achievement (Y. Lee, 1991).

Relative Functionalism

Suzuki (1980) was among the first to present a theory for Asian American educational success that combines elements of the cultural explanation with social and historical explanations. According to his argument, early Asian American immigrants, excluded from labor unions and forced into self-employment, pushed their children toward education in the hopes that they would have better lives. Suzuki also argues that schools rewarded certain cultural traits (e.g., self-discipline, obedience, respect for authority), thereby cementing the aforementioned cultural traits and Asian Americans' belief that education leads to self-improvement and social mobility.

Since very few other options existed, they very likely saw schooling as one of the only avenues left for their children's upward mobility. This almost desperate faith in schooling was undoubtedly reinforced by the traditional veneration accorded to education in Asian societies. The schools, in turn, reaffirmed this faith by rewarding compliance, good behavior, perseverance and docility of Asian children (p. 173).

Suzuki's theory that Asian American educational success is linked to social and cultural factors has been supported by more recent work (Hirschman & Wong, 1986; Mark & Chih, 1982; Sue & Okazaki, 1990). Sue and Okazaki (1990) assert that Asian American educational performance is a "product of cultural values (i.e., ethnicity) and status in society (minority group standing)" (p. 917). They, like Suzuki, found that discrimination in noneducational areas has led Asian Americans to view education as a relatively functional means of upward mobility. However, while this theory offers insight into how culture and minority-group status influence academic achievement among Asian Americans, it still does not address low achievement among Asian Americans.

Cultural Ecologists

In an attempt to understand differential achievement among minority groups, cultural ecologists have pointed to the ways in which identity, historical experiences, and perceptions of opportunities affect school performance (Gibson, 1988; Matute-Bianchi, 1986, 1991; Ogbu, 1978, 1983, 1987, 1989, 1991; Suárez-Orozco, 1989, 1991). Ogbu (1989) distinguishes between what he calls voluntary and involuntary minorities. He defines voluntary minorities as immigrants who voluntarily come to this country (e.g., Asian Americans) in search of a better life and involuntary minorities as those who were incorporated into the United States through slavery or conquest (e.g., African Americans, Mexicans, Hawaiians). Ogbu (1987) argues that differences in achievement levels between voluntary and involuntary minorities are related to their respective perceptions regarding future opportunities and their perceptions and responses to schooling. According to Ogbu, voluntary minorities tend to do well in school because they see schooling as a necessary step to social mobility. They see themselves as guests in the United States who must live by the host's rules. Furthermore, they interpret the cultural and language barriers they face as things they must overcome in order to succeed. In short, Ogbu, like Sue and Okazaki, argues that Asian Americans do well in school because they believe in the connection between school and future success. On the other hand, Ogbu argues that involuntary minorities reject the notion that school success will lead to social mobility. He asserts that, due to persistent economic and social discrimination, involuntary minorities do not believe in the possibility of social mobility. These minorities reject the dominant culture and develop an oppositional culture. Ogbu argues that involuntary minorities underachieve in school because they view schooling as a threat to their oppositional cultures and identities.

Although Ogbu's framework provides important insight into the relationship between a group's perception of schooling and that group's achievement in school, his categories promote the stereotype that Asian Americans are a monolithic group with shared achievement levels and shared attitudes toward schooling. While the cultural-ecological perspective points to significant intergroup differences, it does not uncover the equally significant intragroup differences. One result is that Asian Americans are once again seen as model minorities whose diverse and complex experiences remain hidden.

Like the research of the cultural ecologists, my research suggests that students' identities, perceptions of opportunities, perceptions of schooling, and achievement are linked. However, like the work of Trueba, Cheng, and Ima (1993), my research reveals that there is significant intragroup variability among Asian American students. Asian Americans do not see themselves as being the same; they do not share a common attitude regarding future opportunities or toward schooling. In the remainder of this chapter I examine the relationships among Asian American student identities, attitudes toward schooling, and academic achievement. Each of the four Asian American identity groups at Academic High had a unique perspective on schooling that influenced their experiences. Similarly, Matute-Bianchi (1986, 1991) identified five ethnic-identity subgroups among students of Mexican-descent, each of which developed distinct strategies and accommodations in response to their situations in the United States.

ACHIEVEMENT AMONG
ASIAN AMERICANS AT ACADEMIC HIGH

During my first days of fieldwork at Academic High School, teachers and administrators were eager to show me that their Asian students were doing well (i.e., that they were model minorities). Teachers pointed to the bulletin board in the main corridor, which listed the names (many Asian) of the top ten students in each graduating class in order to show me that Asians did well at Academic High. An overview of such indicators of academic achievement as academic awards and enrollment in advanced placement (AP), honors, and mentally gifted (MG) classes suggested that many Asian Americans at Academic were successful. The class of 1990 had six Asian American students ranked in the top ten, a fact which led Asian and non-Asian students to nickname the class the "Asian class."

Despite the high proportion of Asian students who are at the top of the academic rankings, a thorough examination of the rankings illustrates that not all Asian American students are successful. During the 1988-89 school year, fifteen Asian students were deselected from Academic because of weak academic performance and sent back to their neighborhood schools. Of the eighteen students in the class of 1989 who were deemed ineligible to graduate with their class, three (16%) were Asian. These three students eventually received Academic High diplomas after completing summer school classes. In the class of 1989, four students were deselected from Academic High and transferred back to their neighborhood schools. One Asian American student was among this group. In addition to these students with serious academic troubles, the successful students told me that there were many Asian students who "just get by."

Korean-Identified Students

Korean-identified students believed school success was essential for social mobility in the United States. They worked hard in school and actively pursued information regarding higher education. According to many of these students, success would be a high-paying job in business or as a doctor, lawyer, or engineer. Korean-identified students often stated that their parents decided to come to the United States because of the educational opportunities for them. Some students spoke of the responsibility and guilt they felt for their parents' sacrifices. Others reported that their parents put pressure on them to achieve for the family. In describing the relationship between Korean parents' attitudes and the academic achievement of their children, Eun-Young Kim (1993a) states:

> Korean immigrants consider money and prestige the criteria for success. However, it is when one understands that, for Korean-American immigrant parents, prestige is synonymous with the academic achievement of their children that one begins to understand the relatively high academic achievement of Korean-American students and their disproportionate concentration on certain majors in college and in certain professional careers. (p. 228)

Korean students reported that their parents instructed them to respond to racial prejudice by working hard in school to prove how smart they were. Similarly, in interviews with Chinese American parents, Mark and Chih (1982) found that Chinese American parents instruct their children to ignore racist remarks and to work hard in school in order to show whites how smart Chinese people are. Despite the Korean-identified students' positive attitudes toward schooling, achievement among these students varied. Korean-identified students with limited English proficiency experienced the greatest academic difficulty.

Some Korean-identified students engaged in an informal system of self-help to deal with the Korean-identified students who experienced academic difficulties. Kay Row, a high-achieving, Korean eleventh grader introduced in Chapter 2, explained that she felt it was her responsibility to help younger Korean classmates who had academic problems. She helped younger Korean students with their homework and counseled them about which teachers to take for which classes.

Another way that Korean-identified students responded to differential achievement among Koreans was to promote their image as model minorities/high achievers and to deny the existence of academic problems among Koreans. Jane Park said this to a group of her Korean-identified peers: "American kids have this stereotype like we're smart. We are smarter. I mean, I don't think it's a stereotype. . . . Look at our report cards. We are better and we have to show it." When I mentioned to Jane that I had heard that there were Korean students who were experiencing academic difficulties, she responded by insisting that Koreans were "still smarter than other kids." She and her friends denied the fact that there were Koreans who were experiencing academic difficulties. Jane believed that, by being like model minorities, Koreans could earn the respect of whites, and she silenced any information that she believed might threaten the status of Koreans.

Asian-Identified Students

As pointed out in Chapter 2, like the model minorities described by the media, the Asian-identified students could be found studying before school and during lunch periods. These students stated that their parents had told them that doing well in school was important in order to do well in this country. Asian-identified students dreamt of jobs in medicine, engineering, computer science, or other science-related fields. Like the Korean-identified students, Asian-identified students were motivated to work hard because they felt obligated to their families for the sacrifices they had made. Suárez-Orozco (1989) reports similar achievement motivation among students from Central America. Asian-identified students reported that their parents encouraged them to turn to education as a means of escaping discrimination. Although the students who identified as Asian worked hard and held positive attitudes toward schooling, these students ranged from high achievers to low achievers. Once again, the experience of the low achievers suggests that positive attitudes and hard work do not necessarily guarantee school success.

Profiles of High Achievers. Introduced in Chapter 2, Thai Le ranked third in his class and had always been an exemplary student. Thai took AP and honors classes and earned straight A's. In elementary school, his academic talent had allowed him to skip two grade levels. During his junior year at Academic, his academic prowess won him a full scholarship to participate in a special summer program at Carnegie-Mellon University.

Thai explained that his mother had always encouraged him and his sister to work hard and do well in school. He explained that he did not have any chores around the house because his primary responsibility was to get good grades. Thai's mother, a cosmetology student, dreamt that her children would become white-collar professionals and achieve the American dream. Thai's family had come to the United States as refugees from Vietnam. He told me that his family had lost everything to communism and that he planned to help his family regain their economic security. His plans were to do well in school, win a scholarship to a prestigious university get a good job, and make a lot of money in order to support his parents.

Although Thai's mother had high expectations for her son, she had warned him that, as a Chinese person, he must choose his career carefully. Thai explained that his mother counseled him against a career that would require public speaking because he has a Chinese accent. As noted in Chapter 2, Thai wanted to become a lawyer and a politician, but instead he planned to be an engineer. It should be noted that Thai spoke grammatically correct/standard English and that he was an A student in AP English. Despite his high level of English-language skills, Thai believed that his accent would be a barrier to his success.

Like others who identified as Asian, Mei Mei Wong (introduced in Chapter 2) worked hard in school and believed that her hard work would one day pay off in the form of a good job. By many standards, Mei Mei was a highly successful student. Within five years of coming to the United States, Mei Mei had already earned academic success at an elite American high school. She was ranked in the top ten students in her class, took honors and AP classes, played in the orchestra, and was a member of the softball team. Her academic prowess won her a scholarship to attend a special summer program for students interested in science. Despite her success, Mei Mei was uneasy. In the following quotation, Mei Mei talks about how the model minority stereotype has affected her sense of self:

> They [whites] will have stereotypes, like we're smart. . . . They are so wrong, not everyone is smart. They expect you to be this and that and when you're not. . . . (*shook her head*) And sometimes you tend to be what they expect you to be and you just lose your identity . . . just lose being yourself. Become part of what . . . what someone else want[s] you to be. And it's really awkward too! When you get bad grades, people look at you really strangely because you are sort of distorting the way they see an Asian. It makes you feel really awkward if you don't fit the stereotype.

Mei Mei often worried about whether she would succeed. Her statement illustrates the pressure that the model minority stereotype places on Asian students to achieve and how the stereotype influenced her self-perception. Despite her past success, Mei Mei often talked to her peers about her fear of failure. After exams, Mei Mei would typically announce that she had failed. For Mei Mei, any grade lower than an A was a failing grade. Although Mei Mei's teachers and non-Asian peers tried to reassure her, Mei Mei continued to doubt herself. Because the model minority stereotype sets the parameters for "good" and "acceptable" behavior, students like Mei Mei feared that failure to live up to these standards would mean being perceived as "unacceptable."

Profiles of Low Achievers. Like their high-achieving counterparts, the low-achieving students who identified as Asian worked hard in school and believed that schooling was the key to a secure future. I stumbled upon my first group of low-achieving, Asian-identified students during my initial weeks at Academic. However, since these students fit my stereotype of model achievers rather than my image of academically troubled students, it took me weeks before I realized my discovery.

Ming Chang was one of these seemingly model achievers who turned out to be a low achiever. When I met Ming, he was eating lunch with a group of quiet Asian males. When I arrived at their table, they acknowledged me and then quickly went back to playing chess. Their behavior fed into my stereotype of quiet and studious Asian students. Since they did not talk to me, I decided to tell them a little about my research. They then told me that they were all from Cambodia (ethnic Chinese or Cambodian). Since I had not met many students from Cambodia, I asked them whether they would agree to be interviewed. Although nobody refused, they did not appear to be eager to talk to me.

At the end of their lunch period, Ming lingered for a few moments and then suddenly began to tell me all about his escape from Cambodia and the recent death of his brother. Ming explained that these incidents had sapped him of his energy. It was with this rather dramatic disclosure that Ming and I began our relationship. I followed him to classes and ate lunch with him and his group on a regular basis. Despite all of this contact and the fact that he regularly shared information about how he was feeling, I had little information about his academic achievement. In my mind, Ming was a diligent and successful student.

It was Ming's government teacher, Brian Johnson, who finally told me about Ming's academic problems. Ming was on the verge of failing government, a major course needed for graduation. Mr. Johnson approached me about Ming because he felt that he could not reach him and thought I might have some advice. In his words, "I just don't know what to do. He won't come to [group] tutoring sessions, and he won't come to me for help. We don't have problems personally. . . . In fact, Ming talks to me about his personal problems all of the time." When I spoke to Ming about his problems in government, I learned that he was also failing his English class and that he was having problems in physics. The most surprising fact, however, was not that he was having academic difficulty, but that many of his peers assumed that Ming was academically successful. On at least one occasion a member of the ASA tried to recruit Ming as a tutor for their peer tutoring program.

When I suggested to Ming that he attend the tutoring sessions, Ming shook his head and said that he would not even consider attending these sessions. Ming said that it would be embarrassing to reveal his academic difficulties and that Asians did not talk about their problems. In his words, "You know Asians don't talk about their problems. . . . We just keep it inside. . . . My father would kill me if I talk about stuff." Ming was referring to the Asian ethos which states that an individual's first loyalty is to his or her family and that "bad" behavior (i.e., disclosure of failure) on the part of an individual shames the entire family (Sue & Sue, 1971).

The ironic thing, however, was that Ming often spoke to non-Asians about his personal problems. The stories about his experiences in Cambodia and his experience as a refugee were well known among teachers. Why, then, did Ming feel comfortable sharing these stories and not feel comfortable asking for academic help? In order to answer this question, it is crucial to consider the difference between revealing stories of personal trauma and information about academic problems.

Stories of Cambodia evoked everything from respect to pity from his teachers and non-Asian peers. Refugee stories conform to the image of Asians as long-suffering people who struggle against the odds to achieve. In short, stories of personal struggle support the model minority image depicted by the popular press during this period. These articles ignored Asian American students who have academic problems. Ming and other Asian American students at Academic High were aware of the model minority image depicted in the popular press, and, as I mentioned in Chapter 1, some students spoke specifically about the "Whiz Kid" piece in *Time* (Brand, 1987). I would argue that Ming's reluctance to seek academic support was based in part on his desire to live within the boundaries of the model minority stereotype. Since academic failure clearly contradicts the model minority stereotype, Ming felt that admitting his academic failure would cause his family to lose face (be ashamed). Goffman (1967) writes that the "loss of face" is associated with contradicting approved social attributes. A desire to adhere to traditional Asian values also silenced Ming. In the end, Ming's refusal to seek help for his academic difficulties perpetuated his academic problems and left him feeling isolated and depressed.

Ming's academic problems were related to his difficulties with English. Ming had been in the ESOL program in middle school and during his ninth-grade year at Academic High. Although he was deemed eligible for mainstreaming at the end of the ninth grade, he still had trouble with reading and writing. It is important to point out that Academic High only offered ESOL for ninth graders. At the end of the ninth-grade year, students are evaluated and those not deemed eligible for mainstreaming are deselected and sent back to their neighborhood high school. Those who stay at Academic High could take an elective course designed to help students with reading and writing skills. Students complained that this class was unorganized and not helpful. Later I learned that this course was being taught by a long-term substitute for the semester.

During the remainder of the year I met several Asian-identified students who were having academic difficulties related to their problems with the English language. All had been students in the ESOL program. Like

Ming, these students tended to be rather quiet and hesitant about reaching out for academic support. They explained that they were ashamed of their accents and that they avoided speaking in front of "Americans." On several occasions I observed non-Asian students ridiculing Asian students for their accents. In all of these cases, the comments went unchallenged by the teacher or other students.

Relationships with Teachers

Korean-identified and Asian-identified students were described by their teachers as model students. Teachers appreciated their quiet and polite classroom behavior. Previous studies have suggested that teachers favor Asian students because they perceive Asians to be well behaved and academically competent (Schneider & Lee, 1990; M. G. Wong, 1980). Mr. Cohen, a science teacher, asserted that he liked Asian American students because they were "easy to teach and don't cause any trouble."

Suzuki (1980) argues that Asian American students are favored by their teachers because they exhibit certain cultural characteristics (e.g., obedience, conformity, respect for authority) that schools seek to foster. Furthermore, Suzuki argues that while obedience, conformity, and respect for authority are necessary characteristics for success in lower-level white-collar work, these traits ultimately prevent Asian Americans from entering positions of power.

> The personality traits exhibited by Asian Americans are the result of a socialization process in which the schools play a major role through their selective reinforcement of certain cultural behavior patterns and inculcation of others that are deemed "appropriate" for lower-echelon white-collar workers. (p. 166)

At Academic High I found that Asian American students were rewarded for being quiet, polite, and respectful. On several occasions I learned from teachers that they had given passing grades to Asian American students who had not earned them. In each case, the student who was passed was described as a quiet and polite student. The teachers reported feeling sorry for the student because he or she had been a "good kid." Similarly, in her study on Hmong students, Goldstein (1985) found that Hmong students were promoted to the next grade level based on their behavior rather than on their academic performance. In the process of passing Asian students along on the basis of behavior, teachers at Academic High were encouraging passivity. Additionally, the school was failing in its duty to prepare students academically.

New Wavers

Unlike the students who simply referred to themselves as Asian, the new wave–identified students did not see school as the key to success in the United States. As pointed out in Chapter 2, the new wave students were almost flamboyant in their disrespect for academic achievement. Like the lads in Willis's study (1977), the new wavers refused to conform to the rules required for academic success (e.g., regular attendance, studying). Their primary goals were to get around the school rules and to pass their classes without having to do much work. When asked what they planned to do after high school, most new wavers responded with vague plans to work or attend community college. Although some spoke of getting high-paying jobs, they did not have concrete ideas about how to achieve these goals.

Lee Chau, discussed in Chapter 2, was a typically resistant new wave student. Unlike Ming, Lee's academic problems were not related to problems with English. Lee simply did not go to his classes or do his work. His teachers described him as "bright, but lazy." Ms. Jefferson, his math teacher, said this: "Oh, Lee's a character. He's not like my other Asian students. . . . He's capable of doing better, but he didn't bother to take a test. He's getting a D and his attitude is 'I'm passing.'" This laissez-faire attitude earned him a place in the bottom quarter of his class.

Lee explained that he did not care about his grades at Academic because he did not have any intentions of going on to college. His plans included a stint in the navy, where he would learn a mechanical skill. For Lee, the biggest attraction to the navy, however, was not the vocational training or the idea of serving his adopted country, but the fact that it offered him an opportunity to develop his boxing skills. It should be noted that the model minority stereotype creates an image of Asian men as small and weak, with enormous brains and scrawny bodies. Lee's comment in Chapter 2 about not being a "wimp" and his disparaging remarks about Asians who "can't fight" suggest that he had internalized this stereotype of Asian men. Lee believed that his athletic abilities set him apart from most other Asian males. Lee's rejection of school was influenced by his desire to emphasize his physical strength and his desire to reject the nerd image of Asian men.

Kevin Ng was another new waver who bragged about his low achievement. Kevin was ethnic Chinese from Vietnam. He and his family arrived in the United States when he was in elementary school. During his elementary and middle school years, Kevin had been a high achiever. In elementary school, Kevin received the ultimate legitimation of his intellectual abilities—the mentally gifted label. At Academic High, however,

Kevin adopted a low-maintenance attitude toward his schooling. He went to class only when it was absolutely necessary (tests) or when it struck his fancy, and he did the minimum amount of studying in order to pass his classes.

Kevin often joked that his favorite subject was lunch. In his words, "I never cut lunch!" During the second semester of his senior year, the only classes that Kevin attended on a regular basis were mechanical drawing and Spanish. He explained that he went to mechanical drawing because he liked it and that he went to Spanish in order to "flirt with all the girls." During this same report period, Kevin received grades ranging from a B in mechanical drawing to a D in elementary functions. Kevin proudly reported that he had received a D in elementary functions despite the fact that he had cut this class 40 times.

According to Kevin, the best way to get through school was to do the minimum amount of work and to enjoy the maximum amount of fun. In his opinion, academic high achievers were missing out on the fun. Kevin explained that he was "more relaxed" about school than other Asians were because he knew that there was "more to life than studying." Kevin criticized his Asian peers for not being able to get along with non-Asians. He believed that studying and doing well in school prevented Asians from being accepted by non-Asians. Kevin wanted to be accepted by non-Asians and believed that being less fixated on school would help him. Despite his efforts, I never observed him socializing with any non-Asian students. Kevin spent all of his lunch periods socializing with other Asian males.

Although Ogbu's work provides us with insights into how history, identity, perceptions of opportunities, and attitudes toward schooling are connected, his framework does not explain why these Southeast Asian students resist school while many of their Southeast Asian peers embrace schooling. One crucial difference between the other Asian American students at Academic High and the new wavers was the fact that new wavers were solely oriented toward their peers. I would argue that the peer orientation of new wavers was influenced by the negative experiences they had had with adult authority figures in the United States. For example, new wavers complained of being unfairly hassled by police. In this quotation, a new waver complained about experiences that he and his friends have had with security guards at a local mall:

The security there, I think they're prejudice[d]. So, every time we stand around, not in the way of other people, still they tell us to "move along or else I gonna throw you out." They did not tell the Americans to pass along. They only pay attention to us.

This student is clearly aware that, as an Asian, he is a member of a low-status group with fewer privileges relative to whites. Because of experiences with police and security guards, new wavers come to school suspicious of all authority figures, including teachers. Solomon (1992) asserts that negative experiences with authority outside of school can leave students with latent resistance.

Another theme that recurred among new wave boys was that they began to hate school after they started to attend Academic. In a fit of anger, Phum Ng explained to me that he had been one of the best students at his middle school but was "just a dummy at Academic." Ting Chun, another new waver, said that he hated Academic High because "everyone here is so smart." I would argue that the intense academic competition at Academic High left many students in the position of being "losers." New wavers like Phum and Ting responded to their situations by refusing to participate in the competition. They felt like losers and believed that they could never win. These students simply resisted any behavior that might have helped them in school. Although their behavior may appear to be self-defeating, their analysis of the situation is not far from the truth. At Academic High, seats in the top tracks were limited and therefore the number of "winners" was limited. The underlying message at Academic High was that only the students in the top tracks were truly smart. As a result of this thinking, students in regular classes felt substandard. I also learned that many Asian American and non-Asian students viewed ESOL as a remedial course. One Asian-identified student reported that students thought of the ESOL course as "a class for dummies." Phum, Ting, and many other new wavers had been students in the ESOL program, and they knew how non-Asians viewed them. Given the competitive situation at Academic High, new wavers decided to opt out of the academic competition and concentrate on "being cool."

The new wavers' social experiences with their Asian and non-Asian peers also contributed to their resistance. As noted earlier, new wavers like Lee and Kevin had rather tenuous relations with non-Asians. Kevin hoped that his underachievement might gain him popularity among non-Asians. Experiences with interracial violence led new wavers to question the ability of an education to protect them from physical harm. For example, Lee's experiences at the subway supported his belief that being tough was more important than being smart. In addition to the problems they had with non-Asians, new wavers experienced intra-Asian conflict. The social problems that the new wavers had with their Asian and non-Asian peers further encouraged new wavers to stick to themselves.

Although all of the new wavers expressed antischool attitudes, some new wavers continued to present an accommodating attitude toward their teachers. When these less confrontational new wavers cut their classes, they went to great efforts to provide their teachers with a legitimate-sounding excuse for their absences. Paul Chen, an American-born Chinese student who identified as Chinese American and Asian, worked in the detention office at Academic High and encountered many new wavers. Paul reported that most new wavers who cut their classes played up to their teachers' stereotypes regarding Asian Americans. When I asked the new wavers what they told teachers when they skipped classes, they told me that they used excuses involving their families "because Americans believe it when Asians say that they are helping their families." Dorothy Chin stated that it was common knowledge among new wavers that "teachers accept excuses from Asians that they wouldn't accept from Americans [whites]." Most teachers either believed the students' stories or chose to overlook the lies. Mr. Cohen said this about Asian American students who had attendance problems: "Of course some Asians aren't as good. But even those who cut class—at least they don't flaunt it in your face. They are even respectful about that. Anyway, most of my Asians are good, hardworking students." Cohen's comments reflect the importance he placed on students' respect for authority. He was willing to overlook the new wavers' behavior as long as they treated him with respect.

The more defiant new wave students were less concerned with maintaining good relations with their teachers. They complained that teachers were "anti-Asian." For their part, teachers viewed these new wavers as Asian students who had gone wrong. Teachers described these students as "less Asian." Teachers asserted that these Asian students were being influenced by TV, popular music, and their non-Asian peers. In short, these teachers believed that these students were "becoming too Americanized." Erickson (1987) has written about the importance of trust between teacher and student in creating positive educational experiences. The new wavers did not trust the teachers to be fair, and the teachers did not trust that the new wavers wanted to learn. The experiences that the new wavers had with adults inside and outside school confirmed their negative attitudes toward authority figures. These experiences also reinforced their dependence on one another.

Within the context of Academic High, the resistance of the new wavers is particularly interesting. Why did the new wavers choose to attend Academic High? Given their ambivalent attitudes toward schooling, it would seem that they might have simply stayed at their neighborhood schools rather than taking the time to apply to Academic High. When I asked my new wave informants why they chose to go to Academic High, they all told me that Academic High was "better" and "safer" than the other high schools in the city. New wavers and other Asian American students described other high schools as being dangerous for Asian students. Thus new wavers seemed to be motivated to stay at Academic High by their fear of anti-Asian violence at other high schools.

Asian American–Identified Students

Like the high-achieving Asians, Asian American–identified students worked hard and did well in school. These students were generally in the top academic tracks. Asian American–identified students spoke about studying law, journalism, film, and ethnic studies in college. Unlike the Korean- and Asian-identified students, the Asian American–identified students did not believe that an education would bring them equal standing in the United States. Although they did not accept the rhetoric that education was the great social equalizer, they believed that their lives would be more difficult without an education. Asian American students hoped to use their education to fight racism.

Although all of the Asian American–identified students were high achievers, they rejected the model minority label. They were quick to point out that Asian Americans were a diverse group and that many Asian Americans experienced academic difficulties. In the following quotation, Xuan Nguyen described how the stereotype affected high and low achievers:

> I used to go into classes and if you don't do that well in math or science, the teacher is like, "What are you? Some kind of mutant Asian? You don't do well in math. . . ." You see, I'm not that good in math. I also find that a lot of my friends become upset if they're not good students. . . . I don't think it's right for them to have to feel defensive. And for people who are doing well, it's just like, "Oh, they [Asians] didn't have to work for it . . . they're just made that way."

Xuan took honors-level classes in English, Latin, and social studies and was a student in the mentally gifted program. Additionally, she was one of the first Asian students at Academic High to be a National Merit scholarship semifinalist. Although she was a highly successful student, Xuan understood how the model minority stereotype affected low achievers. As an average math student, Xuan had often been made to feel like a low achiever simply because she did not fit the stereotype of the Asian math genius.

CONCLUSIONS

The English-language difficulties experienced by the low-achieving Korean- and Asian-identified students suggest that Academic High needed to provide additional academic support for non-native English speakers. Although some of the variation in Asian American student achievement can be traced to English-language difficulties, the data presented in this chapter suggest that student identity is also related to achievement. Like Ogbu, I would argue that identity, historical experiences, perceptions regarding future opportunities, and attitudes toward schooling are related. Students in all of the identity groups were aware of their status as minorities. This awareness influenced their attitudes toward schooling. Korean- and Asian-identified students held positive attitudes toward schooling based on their belief that education would help them to achieve social and economic advancement. Both Korean- and Asian-identified students attempted to live up to the model minority standards. They were motivated by a sense of guilt and responsibility to their families. New wave–identified students did not believe in the connection between schooling and future success. They resisted any behavior that encouraged academic achievement. Their resistance challenges the cultural ecological position that, as a group, recent arrivals to the United States hold positive folk theories of success. Students who identified as Asian American were high achievers who worked hard in school. Although they did not believe education would guarantee them equal opportunity, they hoped that education would allow them to more effectively fight social inequalities. The Asian American–identified students' continued efforts in school, despite their perception of racism, challenge the cultural-ecological position that minorities either downplay racism and embrace schooling, or perceive limited opportunities based on racism and resist schooling. Asian American–identified students saw school success as part of their resistance to racism. The cases of the new wave– and Asian American–identified students suggest that students' identities and responses to schooling are constantly being negotiated. Ogbu's exclusive concentration on what students bring to school because of their particular minority status (i.e., voluntary or involuntary) overlooks this fact.

Contrary to the model minority stereotype, Asian American students at Academic High varied in their academic achievement and in their attitudes toward schooling. The stereotype silences the voices of low-achieving students like Ming and Lee. Furthermore, the stereotype silences the complexity of the high-achieving students' experience. In short, the experiences of Asian American students at Academic High highlights the diversity within Asian American communities.

CHAPTER 4

Constructing
Race Relations

> May 17, 1989—I spent the day tailing Teddy Lee. I had a
> particularly interesting conversation with Mr. Thomas, one of
> Teddy's teachers. Mr. Thomas described Asian students as the
> saviors of Academic High. First, he made it a point to tell me
> that "Orientals are my best students." Then, he asserted that the
> school had been "going downhill" until the Asian students started
> coming. According to him, "Orientals are bringing up the scores in
> the school and in the district."

In this chapter I explore the role that Asian American students played in
the construction of race relations at Academic High. First, I look at the current admissions policies and place them within the context of Academic
High's history. Second, I examine competition within the school. One aspect is the intense system of academic sorting and tracking that resegre-
gates students. Another facet is participation in extracurricular activities. I
will look at two high-status extracurricular activities—one that students of
color described as being "all white," and one that a white faculty member
described as being "white and Asian." I argue that the system of intense
competition that surrounds the entire Academic High experience from
admission to graduation creates insiders and outsiders. Furthermore, I
argue that white teachers, counselors, and administrators responded to
the inequality among students by setting Asian Americans up as model
minorities and using them as evidence that equal opportunity existed for
all races to succeed at Academic High. Those who saw Asian Americans as
model minorities held to the belief that race is equal to ethnicity. According to this perspective, success among white ethnics, like success among
Asian Americans, proves that the system is open (Omi & Winant, 1986). By
describing Asian Americans as model minorities, white faculty and staff
pit Asian Americans against African Americans and against all students
who were outsiders at Academic High School (AHS). Although the school

played a role in fueling interracial tension between Asian Americans and other students of color, most white teachers and administrators denied the very existence of interracial tension at the school.

ADMISSIONS

From its inception in the 1830s, Academic High has enjoyed a reputation as a prestigious and special institution. Within the city, Academic High is known as a training ground for future doctors, lawyers, judges, and captains of industry. The prestige associated with the Academic High diploma is based on the school's image as a highly competitive school.

Founded during the common schools era, Academic High reflected the tension between the public (i.e., republicanism's concern for community) and private (i.e., capitalist) interests that characterized that period (Labaree, 1988). Academic High's founders sought to resolve the tension through the institutionalization of meritocracy. It was decided that admission to Academic High would be open to any boy who proved his academic worth on the standardized entrance exam. The rhetoric was that exclusivity would be based on merit, not on birth. It must be pointed out, however, that girls were excluded from the competition "by birth." The group most interested in sending their children to Academic High were members of the middle class whose economic status was being threatened by industrialization (Labaree, 1988). The limited number of spaces in each graduating class and the meritocratic competition to gain admission made an Academic High diploma a scarce and valuable property, and middle-class parents fought to get their sons into Academic High.

Academic High enjoyed its elite status until the 1970s, when enrollment and scholastic achievement plummeted. Admission to Academic High became less selective in order to maintain enrollment. During this period the middle classes were leaving the public schools and Academic High was forced to lower its admission standards in order to maintain its enrollment. Many faculty members mentioned that the 1970s and early 1980s were marked by an increase in African American students and working-class Italian American students from the south side, and many teachers suggested that there was a cause-and-effect relationship between this change and lowered achievement. Mrs. White, a 21-year veteran of Academic High, lamented that "students went downhill—particularly in the late 1960s and 1970s with the riots." Teachers like Mrs. White were bitter about the decline of Academic High's prestige during this era. They believed that Academic High's elite status was based on its ability to exclude, and they feared that a more diverse population threatened the school. Holtz's (1989) data on faculty attitudes regarding changes in Academic's student population confirm this. She quotes one faculty member on the impact of white flight on Academic High:

> They [Jewish students] were kids who put a great premium on learning. They came from families which emphasized education as the summum bonum in their lives. . . . In the late 70s and early 80s there was a move out of the city on the part of the more ambitious, the more motivated, and there was at this point no replacement. (p. 98)

During the early 1980s a few female students fought to gain admission to Academic High. Academic High alumni waged a bitter battle against the admission of girls. When the first female students won the right to attend Academic High in 1983, the history of Academic High was changed forever. The first female students arrived at Academic High in September of 1983, and Dr. Levine, the current principal, arrived in January of that same academic year. Unlike the man whom the alumni favored to become the principal, Levine was not a graduate of Academic High School. Like the girls, Levine came to Academic High as an outsider. Ironically, the admission of girls and Levine's tenure have been credited with Academic High's resurgence as an elite institution. Levine took it upon himself to restore Academic High to its former status. Upon his arrival, Levine dismissed 400 students who were experiencing academic difficulties and reinstated old admissions policies (Labaree, 1988). Under Levine, the standards for admission are all A's and B's, with one C allowed in the seventh and eighth grades, and standardized test scores (math and English) at or above the 85th percentile. Students who are unable to maintain satisfactory performance face "deselection" (transfer back to their neighborhood comprehensive high school). Students who fail three academic subjects are recommended for transfer, and students who fail two academic subjects for a second year are automatically deselected. Levine asserted that anyone who worked hard enough and had the talent should be welcomed at Academic High; he also implied that students who could not meet the standards should not be at Academic High. In short, he spoke the language of equal opportunity and meritocracy. Through his actions, he sent the message out that the years of decline were over and that Academic High's elite status was once again secure. Levine's success in returning Academic High to its elite position won him the support of alumni and the majority of the faculty.

In describing the upward trend of Academic High, Levine said this, "When I came here enrollment was down to 1,000. There are over 2,000 students in the building now. When I came here there was one National Merit semifinalist. There were 19 this year out of a total of 28 in the entire district." Levine's tacit suggestion was that before he arrived at Academic

High, the school had reached an all-time low. The students who made up the class of 1993 came from more than 200 junior high schools. There were 2,542 applicants for the class of 1993, and 950 students (37%) were accepted for admission. Levine was quick to point out that there were students attending Academic High who lived outside of the school district and paid tuition in order to attend. During my research, the subject of the growing student population led some teachers to speculate about the building of additions or the moving of the school to a larger building.

Despite the fact that the alumni and most teachers were pleased with Levine's success in returning Academic High to its former glory, not everyone favored his methods. Levine's exclusionary policies came at a cost to some students. As noted earlier, Levine had 400 students dismissed from AHS because of low achievement. Levine's critics charge that his policies have hurt African American, male students. Among African American students and staff, there was a common perception that African American, male students were unwelcome at Academic High.

In 1976 African American males made up 43% of the total student population at AHS. In 1989 the African American student population made up 35% of the total student population at AHS. While the percentage of African American students dropped in the 1980s, the percentage of Asian American students increased. For example, during the 1982–83 school year Asian Americans constituted 8.6% of Academic's total student population. When I began fieldwork at Academic, Asian Americans made up 18% of the total student population at Academic. The increase in the percentage of Asian American students at AHS reflected an increase in the total number of Asian American students in the school district and a change in the entrance requirements at AHS.

During his first years at AHS, Levine instituted new policies that greatly increased Asian American student enrollment. First, he established Academic High's first ESOL classes. Then, he made an exception to the admissions policy for limited English proficiency (LEP) students. The requirement of scoring at the 85th percentile on the English section of the standardized exam was waived for non-native speakers of English who had been in the United States for three years or less. Instead, a minimum score of the 50th percentile was set for ESOL applicants on the English section of the citywide exam. Although the standards for English were lowered for ESOL students, they were expected to have higher math scores than non-ESOL students The ESOL teacher, Dr. Rafferty, worked with Levine to screen the ESOL applicants. Students accepted under the ESOL policy enrolled in the ESOL class for ninth graders. As noted earlier, at the end of the ninth-grade year, students are evaluated for mainstreaming, and those who are found ineligible are sent back to their neighborhood high school.

According to Levine, these changes were made in order to ensure that the best and brightest students from all backgrounds would feel welcomed at Academic High. Levine explained that his policy on ESOL students respected the fact that non-native speakers were disadvantaged by the old system. He argued that it was discriminatory to hold a non-native speaker up to the same standards as a native speaker. In his words, "The ESOL policy gives bright kids who haven't been in the country for very long a chance." He went on to explain that the higher math score required for ESOL students ensured that non-native speakers did not get an unfair advantage over other students. Furthermore, he argued that in the case of non-native speakers, high math scores were the best evidence of a student's academic potential. Levine asserted that the "perfect ESOL applicant scored at the 74th percentile on the English section and at the 99th percentile on the math section." Although the ESOL program and admissions policies are open to all LEP students, during my research, Asian American LEP students made up the majority of ESOL acceptances. The acceptance rate for Asian American students for the class of 1993 was 40% as compared to the overall acceptance rate of 37.3%. It should also be pointed out that not all Asian American students at AHS were accepted under the ESOL policies. Asian American students reported that most of their non-Asian peers and many of their teachers assumed that all Asian Americans were ESOL admits.

The increase in the Asian American student population has not gone unnoticed. Some have described Levine's ESOL policy as his active recruitment of Asian American students. This perception extends beyond the AHS community. For example, while I was first searching for a research site, a teacher at another public high school in the city suggested that I consider AHS because "the principal is recruiting Asians." Critics charged that Levine's policies give preferential treatment to Asian Americans. A few suggested that Asian Americans who "can't speak English" didn't deserve to be at Academic High. Some teachers accused Levine of recruiting Asian American students to fulfill a quota for minority students. They claimed that Levine was "recruiting" Asians in order to avoid African American students. Others asserted that Levine made exceptions for Asian Americans because he assumed that Asian Americans were good students. Furthermore, they charged that Levine held higher expectations for Asian Americans than for African Americans and other minorities.

Mr. Fox, an African American teacher, stated that he feared that "Asians were replacing blacks at Academic." Mr. Fox also asserted that ESOL should be open to African American students who speak black English. Although he supported ESOL for Asian LEP students, he claimed that excluding African American speakers of black English from ESOL denied them equal opportunity.

I think ESOL for Asians with English problems is great! In fact, I think ESOL should include black students. We expect Asians' deficiencies will be something they grow out of, but blacks are not expected to succeed. Many of them [blacks] come from homes where they don't speak standard English. We should recognize this and give them extra help, too!

Mr. Fox argued that having lower expectations for African American students was racist, and he feared that the lowered expectations contributed to African American student underachievement at Academic High. He suggested that the exclusion of African Americans from ESOL was part of a general racism against African Americans at Academic.

Mr. Fox stated that, as an African American teacher, he was not immune to the racism present in the school, and he suggested that things were much worse for his African American students. According to Mr. Fox, phrases such as the "good old days" or the "old Academic" were a racist code for the days when the school was dominated by Eastern European Jews. He explained that he chose to eat in his classroom rather than enter the faculty cafeteria and listen to the racism of the white faculty: "There's racism on the faculty. . . . I don't eat in the lunchroom because I'm sick of hearing racist things about what Academic was like in the 'good old days.'"

The primary concern of Mr. Fox was for the African American male students at AHS. Several times he told me that "black males are the group most likely to drop out of Academic." He reported that over 50% of the students who are deselected from AHS are African American males and that African American males at Academic were an "endangered species." He warned his African American male students that they might become an "extinct animal" if they were not careful. Fox also blamed coeducation for hurting African American males at AHS. He asserted that African American males were "easily co-opted" and that "whenever girls were involved, black male achievement went down."

Levine and his supporters believed that students of all races had an equal opportunity to gain admission to AHS. They believed in the fairness and neutrality of the meritocratic system. As such, they believed that any decrease in the percentage of African American students at AHS was the result of chance. Levine also adamantly denied the rumors that there were quotas for minorities. Furthermore, he reminded his critics that ESOL was open to all LEP students and that ESOL students must score higher on the math section of the citywide exam than other applicants.

Although Levine denied a conspiracy to recruit Asians, many of Levine's supporters, as well as his critics, believed that he was recruiting Asian Americans. One counselor made this comment, "The boss wants them [Asian students] here—And why shouldn't he? He's prize-oriented, award-oriented, and our Asians do well." Not only did this counselor believe that Levine recruited Asian American students, but she asserted that he was justified in doing so. She suggested that Asian Americans had "saved" Academic High and that Asians were "replacing Jews at the top." Interestingly, her comments point to how Asians and Jews are often similarly stereotyped as good students (i.e., model minorities). In sum, I would argue that whether Levine did or did not recruit Asian American students became less significant than the fact that most of Levine's detractors and his supporters believed that he did. The belief that Levine recruited Asians influenced race relations between African Americans and Asians.

CREATING INSIDERS AND OUTSIDERS

As noted earlier, the competition at Academic High creates insiders and outsiders. While insiders enjoy status, privilege, and a sense of security, outsiders experience insecurity regarding their status. Outsiders can gain insider status through high academic achievement and participation in prestigious extracurricular activities. At Academic High, African American students, working-class Italian American students, and Asian American students struggle to overcome their outsider status. I will argue that students who perceive themselves to be outsiders feel that they must compete against one another for insider status.

Tracking

Upon entering Academic High, students are scrutinized by teachers and counselors, and divided into academic tracks. The highest track includes advanced placement classes in which students theoretically do college-level work and take the College Board's AP exams. AP classes are popular among students who hope that a high score on the AP exam will earn them college credit and exempt them from introductory courses in college. Within AP classes, students are further separated into those who are chosen by the teachers to sit for the AP exam and those who are discouraged from taking the exam. One student remarked on his AP science teacher's policy of selecting students to take the AP exam: "He discourages his weaker students from taking the test. That way the percentage of 4's and 5's [5 = highest possible score] were guaranteed to be inflated." According to the new rules for the 1989–90 school year, all students enrolled in AP classes must sit for the College Board's AP exam.

The next highest track includes star classes, which are the equivalent of honors classes. The third level in the academic hierarchy is the regular track. Academic High does not have a remedial track, but students in the regular track report that they feel as though they are in the remedial track. The one "remedial" program is the ninth-grade ESOL, program for non-native speakers of English admitted under the special ESOL rules. According to Levine, all of the ESOL students who have successfully completed the ESOL class during the last five years have been deemed qualified for mainstreaming.

A final category into which students are separated is the mentally gifted program. This program is open only to students who have been identified by the school district as mentally gifted. While many students in the MG program take AP and star classes, the MG program offers special classes in everything from math and English to a class in current events. Special teachers are designated as MG mentors who teach MG classes and serve as special guidance counselors to the MG students. Special MG rooms exist where students go to do homework and to socialize.

The quintessential example of Academic's dedication to competition among students, however, is the fact that students are ranked according to their grade-point average after the tenth-, eleventh-, and twelfth-grade years. The top 25 students are considered to be a special elite. At graduation, the top 10 students are singled out for special mention. In calculating grade-point averages, classes are weighted (e.g., AP classes receive the highest points). This method of calculating grade-point averages gives the top-tracked students a negotiated advantage of coming out on top.

While admission to Academic High grants all students a certain amount of prestige, the highest kudos are reserved for those who win places in the top tracks. Students are told that they are the best in the city because they got into Academic High, but the implicit message is that not all students are equal. Within the hierarchical culture of Academic High School, academic success is highly prized and is one of the most important ways for outsiders to gain insider status. As noted earlier, the special status of Academic hinges on its real and perceived academic excellence. Thus students who do well on standardized exams (e.g., SAT, PSAT, citywide exam) help promote Academic's image as an academically elite school. In general, high-achieving students, regardless of race, are welcomed by the faculty and staff.

Critics of tracking have noted that tracking is often a substitute for racial segregation and that this practice is particularly striking at selective public high schools (Oakes, 1985). A look at the academic rankings for the class of 1989 and the class of 1990 reveals that the majority of students in the top ranks are white and Asian. For example, in 1989, 86 students graduated as distinguished students. Of these 86 students, 65% were white, 21% were Asian, and 13% were African American. In 1990, 93 students graduated as distinguished students. Of these 93, 44% were white, 38% were Asian, and 16% were African American. Seats in the star and AP classes were also filled primarily by white and Asian students. According to my observations, African American students made up 10% or less of the students in most of the higher-track classes. For example, in my observations of one AP science class, I counted 12 Asian students, 4 white students, and 2 African American students. In my observations of an eleventh-grade star social science class, I counted 8 Asian students, 18 white students, and 3 African American students. The prestigious Book Awards, given to members of the junior class who demonstrate academic excellence and community service, were given to 7 Asian students, 3 white students, and 1 African American student. With the exception of the MG computer lab, where white and Asian boys congregated, the overwhelming majority of students who socialized in the MG room were white. The MG newspaper staff was predominately Jewish and Asian, a fact that led the faculty sponsor and students to joke that the MG paper was essentially the "Asian club, part 2."

Despite the fact that the tracks were racially segregated, tracking as a system went unquestioned by the majority of the faculty and staff. Most white teachers and administrators believed that tracking was necessary in order to best serve the diversity of student levels. They believed that the tracking system was based on fair and neutral principles. Furthermore, they argued that tracking reflected the meritocratic ideals of the school. Dr. Levine promoted the notion of meritocracy at school assemblies and other gatherings for students. During the ceremony marking the promotion of the class of 1990 to senior status, Levine reported on the number of students in the class of 1989 who were not going to be allowed to graduate with their class and argued that it was up to the students to guarantee that the 478 students in the class of 1990 all graduated.

One result of this unquestioning acceptance of meritocracy was that the underrepresentation of African American students in the top tracks was seen as the fault of the African American students themselves. White teachers and counselors suggested that if African Americans were underrepresented in the top tracks, it was because they were lazy or because they lacked the academic talent or interest. Mrs. Ramsey, a white guidance counselor, said this regarding achievement of African American students: "Asians like U of P [University of Pennsylvania], MIT, Princeton. They tend to go to good schools. I wish our blacks would take advantage of things instead of sticking to sports and entertainment." In one brief statement, Mrs. Ramsey reified the model minority stereotype of Asian

Americans and blamed African American students for their situation. According to her perspective, Asian American success was proof that anyone regardless of race could succeed if they put in the proper effort. Her stereotype of African Americans as athletes and entertainers contributed to her belief that African American student underachievement was a result of poor choices. This type of race thinking pitted Asian American students against African Americans.

Although the majority of teachers at AHS believed that equal opportunity existed at AHS, there were teachers who spoke out against the System. Mrs. Lewis, an African American English teacher, was one of the few to voice an opinion regarding student relations that contradicted the image painted by the majority of teachers. The following excerpt from my fieldnotes of June 6, 1989, illustrates her view of Academic:

> *Mrs. Lewis*: Now, have you found many cross-racial relationships?
> *SL*: A few. . .
> *Mrs. Lewis*: Very few. . . . Do you think this place is polarized? Do you think the faculty is doing something to keep this place polarized?
> *SL*: Do you mean tracking?
> *Mrs. Lewis*: Tracking within tracking. And you know, it's not supposed to be like that . . . all of our kids should be in star and AP.

Mrs. Lewis's statement regarding "tracking within tracking" was a reference to the fact that students are sorted and tracked before they enter AHS and are then sorted and tracked again upon acceptance to AHS. Because of its strict admissions policies, which limit admission to those who demonstrate academic excellence, AHS is essentially the highest-track high school within the school district. Mrs. Lewis suggested that academic tracking at AHS was redundant at best and discriminatory at worst. She believed that all students at AHS should have access to the elite curriculum offered to students in the top tracks. Criticism regarding the strict tracking system at AHS was also voiced by Ms. Bergstrom, a white computer science teacher. Ms. Bergstrom was particularly angered by the growing MG program, which she believed was a divisive force in the school. She stated that she was frustrated because Academic High was "becoming two separate schools—one MG and one regular." Bergstrom asserted that the MG program provided a full range of special support for MG students, and she stressed that all students at AHS should have access to these services. Both Ms. Bergstrom and Mrs. Lewis were very concerned about the fact that tracking resulted in the resegregation of African American students into the lower tracks.

When Mrs. Lewis finished talking to me, she introduced me to a student named Keesha Fox and said that I should speak to her regarding cross-racial relations at Academic. Keesha told me that Mrs. Lewis was her role model and had helped her deal with identity problems she experienced as an African American at Academic. She explained that, prior to getting to know Mrs. Lewis, she was very confused about her identity and often felt like she wanted to be white. During my interview with Keesha, she also spoke about the underrepresentation of African American students in the top ranks. Keesha reported that she was always one of the few African Americans in the top tracks and that she felt a lot of pressure to do a good job in order to represent other African American students. The experience of high-achieving African American students at elite high schools deserves further attention. However, since my study focused on Asian American students, I did not pursue this issue.

High-Status Extracurricular Activities

Extracurricular activities serve important social functions in high schools. They provide students with opportunities to develop leadership skills and to jockey for status and position (Eckert, 1989). Academic High sponsors a range of extracurricular activities, but not all are created equal. Participation in high-status extracurricular activities confers high status on students. In this section, I examine the politics surrounding participation on the school newspaper and in the school's music program.

The **Academic Blazer.** Participation on the school newspaper is among the extracurricular activities most respected by the faculty, administration, and alumni, and one that gained students legitimation/insider status. Established in 1923, the *Academic Blazer* is well written and represents the work of some of Academic's best students. Members of the newspaper staff are generally strong academic students who are also active in other school activities. As Karen, a member of the newspaper staff, said, "We're good students, but we aren't nerds. We get involved in other things." The members of the *Academic Blazer* staff are similar to the student type of body leaders that Eckert (1989) calls "jocks."

Among the general student population, members of the newspaper staff are known as the pre-yuppie crowd. The adjectives used to describe the group are *white, middle-class,* and *politically liberal.* Students of color told me that they thought the *Blazer* was an exclusive/white social clique.

Several minority students who had been on the *Blazer* staff stated that they did not feel welcome at staff meetings. While most of the students on the staff were white, there were two notable exceptions: Virginia Hsu, an

ABC who was selected as the 1989 editor, and Kay Rowe, a Korean student who was selected to be the 1989 copy editor. The faculty advisor, Mr. Kraft, interpreted Kay's and Virginia's presence on the staff as proof that the paper is accessible to students of all races. When I asked him what he thought about the image of the paper as an exclusively white activity, he suggested that the underrepresentation of African American students on the staff was due to a lack of talent or interest among African American students. In his words, "We just haven't been able to attract any black students, and the ones we've had have been a disappointment." According to Mr. Kraft, Virginia and Kay proved that participation on the newspaper is not reserved for whites only.

While Kraft and others held Kay and Virginia up as evidence that the paper was open to students of all races, they did not recognize that Kay and Virginia represented exceptions within the Asian American student population. Virginia socialized exclusively with white students and often denigrated Asians in order to gain the acceptance of her white peers. On the other hand, Kay tried to socialize in both the white world of the school newspaper and with her Korean peers, and she experienced tensions with both groups. This issue is discussed further in Chapter 5. The social realities and difficulties that Kay and Virginia faced were not commonly known. Instead, Mr. Kraft and other white teachers used the fact that Kay and Virginia were in positions of power on the paper as evidence that Asians have succeeded in breaking into the white world of the school paper. In addition, they used Kay's and Virginia's "success" to blame African Americans for their absence on the newspaper. In short, Asian Americans via Kay and Virginia were represented as model minorities. Furthermore, Kraft maintained that academic ability and interest, not race, influenced the participation patterns of the newspaper staff.

Although Kraft and the white students on the *Blazer* staff believed that access to the *Blazer* clique was open to all students, African American and some Asian American–identified students told a different story. Jackie Brown, the president of the Black Student Union (BSU), had been on the staff of the *Academic Blazer* but dropped out because she felt unwelcome. She described her experience like this:

> I was like one of the few minorities on the staff . . . I didn't stay with the *Academic Blazer* because I didn't really—I don't know if you would say they didn't give me much respect or give me much to do. . . . Anyways, I didn't fit in too well. From what I can see, people just pull in their friends. They don't just reach out to everyone and say "hey, work on the school paper."

Xuan Nguyen, an Asian American–identified student introduced in Chapter 2, had worked on the staff of the paper. Xuan asserted that members of the *Blazer* were "subtle racists" who spoke the language of equality but refused to listen to the concerns of minority students. She complained that the *Blazer* clique continually denied her experiences and the experiences of all minorities.

The Music Program. The faculty and administration are exceptionally proud of their music program. Each year the music department holds several evening concerts as well as a number of smaller recitals in the library. Students in both the instrumental and choral music programs could be found practicing in the music room throughout the day. Many music students used the music rooms as their study halls and lunchrooms.

I spent a fair amount of time in the music room because I found that Korean-identified students often gathered in Mrs. Clark's office, as explained in Chapter 2. Although I counted mostly white and Korean students in the instrumental music program, I didn't think much about the relative absence of African Americans. The first indication that race was an issue in the music program came about when the Gospel Choir performed in the spring. Without any prompting, Mr. Kadinsky, one of the members of the music department, began to complain about the Gospel Choir. First, he announced that he had a "white and Asian department," and then he claimed that the Gospel Choir was a black "separatist group" that hurt school spirit. He claimed that the BSU and the Gospel Choir fostered separatism and that separatism was becoming a "problem throughout the school."

Kadinsky maintained that students of all races had an equal opportunity to become involved in the instrumental and choral divisions of the music program. He suggested that the presence of Asian students in his program supported his belief. The reality, however, was that there was little diversity among the Asian Americans in his program. Most of the Asian American students in the instrumental music program were either Korean, Taiwanese, or American-born Chinese, and they were all middle-class. The few Southeast Asians in the music department were in choral music. One day while I was observing in the music room, Kadinsky approached me and pointed to a African American male student and said, "Now, he's a talented musician [who is] above the pettiness." Kadinsky seemed to be suggesting that this African American student was a "good black student," different from the African Americans who insisted on separating themselves. African American legal scholar Patricia Williams (1991) argues that African Americans who accept white standards are accepted by whites as being "good blacks," while those who reject white standards are branded as "bad." "Blacks who refuse the protective shell of white goodness and insist that they are black are inconsistent with the paradigm of goodness, and therefore they are bad" (p. 11). Kadinsky seemed to be suggesting that the African American students who insist on being in the Gospel Choir are being "petty." In other words, these African American students have fallen from grace. Kadinsky volunteered that he thought clubs like the ASA and the KSA were "OK" because they provided important support for minorities and encouraged students to blend into the school. On the other hand, he suggested that the Gospel Choir and the BSU encouraged segregation.

The Gospel Choir was formed in 1987. During its first year there were 30 members, and within three years there were 140 members. Mrs. Carter, an African American secretary in the main office, has served as the choir director since the group's beginning. Mrs. Carter saw herself as a role model for the African American students. Students informed me that the group formed in order to sing music that expressed their African American heritage. The group enjoyed a great deal of popularity among all students as well as among the larger African American community, and their concerts were well attended.

After I finished my fieldwork at AHS a situation concerning the Gospel Choir brought the issue of black-white tension out into the open at AHS. The school district ruled that the Gospel Choir was a religious organization and banned the group from practicing and performing on school grounds. In backing up their position, the school district cited the Equal Access Act, which states that religious groups can meet on public school grounds only if there is no school sponsorship. In the case of the Gospel Choir, Mrs. Carter's role as the group's director was seen as school district sponsorship. The school district suggested that Mrs. Carter resign as the director, but Carter and the African American students rejected that suggestion. The district also suggested that the choir broaden its repertoire to include non-Gospel music. African American students and their parents argued that Gospel music is cultural, not religious. They cited the importance of Gospel music throughout African American history. The controversy between the Gospel Choir and the school district, over whether the Gospel Choir is a religious or cultural organization, points to the significance of historical experiences and social position in how groups interpret their social reality.

During my fieldwork, teachers like Kadinsky seemed more troubled by the fact that the Gospel Choir had a distinct identity separate from the homogenized identity supported by the school than by whether or not the group was religious. White teachers asserted that they wanted students of all colors to integrate into the fabric of the school. I would argue that when teachers spoke about "integration," they often meant the assimilation of other cultures into the dominant culture. For teachers like Kadinsky, an all–African American group was antithetical to integration. Interestingly, Asian-identified and Asian American–identified students were fans of the Gospel Choir. Mei Mei Wong asserted that she thought that the ASA needed a similar type of group in order to bring Asians together. Perhaps the school feared that groups like the Gospel Choir might inspire other ethnic and racial groups to follow their lead and form groups that the school perceived as separatist.

"Equal Opportunity" and the Use of the Model Minority

In each of the examples discussed, white teachers, counselors, and administrators responded to evidence of racial imbalance/racial inequality by promoting the idea of equal opportunity. Fine (1991) reminds us that there is a significant gap between equal access and equal outcomes. She writes, "In urban areas, especially for low-income African-American and Latino youths, public schools may offer everyone *access* in, but once inside the doors of public schools, many low-income youths are virtually *disappeared*" (p. 24; emphasis in original). At AHS, white teachers, counselors, and the principal asserted that students of all races had a fair chance to gain admission to AHS, to do well academically, and to participate in extracurricular activities. They believed that the meritocratic system was fair, neutral, and color-blind. Unequal outcomes (i.e., high rate of African American student failure) were often silenced. When forced to face the reality of unequal outcomes, white teachers and administrators explained unequal outcomes as the natural result of differences in student talent, interest, and effort.

Furthermore, white teachers and administrators suggested that the "success" of Asian American students served as evidence that the system was color-blind. In other words, "if Asians [a racial minority] can succeed, then anyone can." It is interesting to note that while the faculty and staff promoted a race/color-blind image of the system, they used a racial minority to prove their point. Takagi (1992) has argued that in the 1980s neoconservatives used similar tactics in their attacks on affirmative action. Neoconservatives asserted that Asian Americans were good/qualified students who were discriminated against by affirmative action policies that overlooked merit in favor of diversity. These neoconservative critics, like the white teachers at AHS, believed that merit was color-blind.

> Although neoconservatives advocated a color-blind system of admissions, they did so by first drawing attention to racial differences in academic achievement and admission. Highlighting the achievements of Asians as a racial minority neoconservatives used Asian American students as an

important racial wedge in the debate in order to criticize institutions for favoring blacks at the expense of Asians and whites. (Takagi, 1992, p. 120)

Thus neoconservatives represented Asian Americans as model minorities who were victimized by affirmative action. Similarly, Asian Americans at AHS were held up as model minorities who achieved success in the admissions process, the tracking process, and high-status extracurricular activities. According to Mr. Kraft, Mrs. Ramsey, and others at AHS, Asian American students represented hard work, individual effort, and talent. The promotion of Asian Americans as model minorities also led to blaming African Americans for their problems. Mrs. Ramsey's suggestion that African American students should "take advantage of things instead of sticking to sports and entertainment" is one example of this victim blaming.

Similarly, some white teachers at AHS suggested that the interests of African Americans were inherently opposed to the interests of Asian Americans. These teachers argued that while Asians gained success through sheer merit, African Americans gained their status through affirmative action. White teachers attempted to engage me in conversations about affirmative action in order to gauge my politics. The following excerpt from my fieldnotes of May 25, 1989, is one such example:

> Mr. Cohen and I were talking about sports when out of the blue he started to question me on my views regarding affirmative action. He said, "What do you think about all these affirmative action programs?" I started off by telling him that affirmative action programs were important because they looked out for diversity and made up for past injustices. When I finished, he told me that he thought affirmative action programs were "unfair because lower ability blacks often get into schools over whites and Asians."

On another occasion, while I was walking down the hall with Thai Le, Mr. Edwards stopped Thai to tell him that he was going to a scholarship banquet for minority students. Thai, who was ranked third in his class, remarked that he had not heard anything about the banquet and demanded to know why he had been left out. Mr. Edwards shot back, "Don't you know you're not a real minority?" Mr. Edwards went on to say that only African Americans and Hispanics were minorities and that they were favored by affirmative action programs that hurt Asians. After sharing this information with Thai, Mr. Edwards turned to me and said that he did not have anything against African Americans. He stated that he was simply offended by policies which gave "anyone free rides" and hurt hardworking individuals. In short, his argument was that he was not antiblack, but simply pro-individual rights. As if to prove that he was not racist, Mr. Edwards used Asian Americans as an example of a group being hurt by affirmative action. Mr. Edwards believed that Asian American interests were represented by meritocratic policies and African American interests were represented by affirmative action and nonmeritocratic practices. According to him, the only "fair" policy would be one based on meritocracy. This teacher's construction of fairness and equality reflects the neoconservative thinking that emerged during the 1970s and took hold in the 1980s (Omi & Winant, 1986). In describing the politics of neoconservatives, Apple (1993) writes:

> The coalition has partly succeeded in altering the very meaning of what it means to have a social goal of equality. The citizen as "free" consumer has replaced the previously emerging citizen as situated in structurally generated relations of domination. Thus, the common good is now to be regulated exclusively by the laws of the market, free by competition, private ownership, and profitability. (p. 34)

Mr. Edwards argued that affirmative action programs were unfair and that an open system of competition would be fair to all who "worked hard." As I reflect on Mr. Edwards's attack on affirmative action, I am struck by how attitudes like his have become dominant now in the mid-1990s.

TEACHERS' INTERPRETATION OF RACE AS ETHNICITY

According to Omi and Winant (1986), the predominant discourse of race in the United States equates race with ethnicity and culture. One of the assumptions of the ethnicity paradigm is that equal opportunity exists (Frankenberg, 1993; Omi & Winant, 1986; Rizvi, 1993; Sleeter, 1993). In her critique of ethnicity theory, Sleeter (1993) states, "Ethnicity theory holds that the social system is open and that individual mobility can be attained through hard work. Over time ancestry will disappear as a determinant in life chances" (p. 160). Omi and Winant (1986) argue, however, that the ethnicity paradigm does "not appreciate the extent to which racial inequality differ[s] from ethnic inequality" (p. 16).

At Academic High, most white teachers interpreted race through the ethnicity paradigm. These teachers (who identified themselves as children of European immigrants) explained that their parents had come to the United States with very little and that through sheer hard work and determination they had achieved social mobility. They spoke of parents who had made enormous sacrifices so that they could go to college.

Furthermore, they reasoned that their personal success proved that equal opportunity existed for everyone.

Jewish teachers attempted to establish co-membership with me over the "similarities between Asians and Jews." They asserted that Jews and Asians came from cultures that encouraged school achievement. They also suggested that other groups (i.e., African Americans) came from cultures that failed to stress the importance of education and therefore African Americans did poorly in school. One day, Mr. Cohen approached me in the halls and cheerfully suggested that I write a book on Asian child-rearing practices for non-Asians. He maintained that there was a tremendous need for such a book and that I could "make a fortune off the book." I told him that I did not consider myself qualified to write such a book, since I never had any interest in research on child rearing and did not even have children of my own. He shrugged off my protests and suggested that I could reflect on my own upbringing. Although he had never asked me about my upbringing, he assumed that I had been raised in a "traditional Asian" fashion.

Teachers and administrators at Academic High believed that many of the problems faced by racial minorities were due to cultural differences. For example, the ESOL teacher, Dr. Rafferty, believed that many of the problems faced by Asian students were due to cultural differences between Asians and non-Asians. Rafferty described himself as a cultural interpreter for Asian students. Teachers, counselors, and Dr. Levine saw Rafferty as the "Asian expert," and his opinions carried a significant amount of weight. Levine always consulted with Rafferty on matters related to Asian American students. In fact, in my first meeting with Levine, in which I presented my proposal for research, he invited Rafferty to join us and to give his opinion.

As noted previously, this vision of race denies the existence of structural barriers to achievement (Omi & Winant, 1986; Rizvi, 1993; Sleeter, 1993). It denies the reality of subordination due to skin color, and it denies the fact that white people experience white skin privilege. Finally, it blames the victims for their problems. In their critique of the ethnicity-equals-race paradigm, Omi and Winant (1986) write:

> Everything is mediated through "norms" internal to the group. If Chicanos don't do well in school, this cannot even hypothetically be due to low-quality education; it has instead to do with Chicano values. After all, Jews and Japanese Americans did well in inferior schools, so why can't other groups? Ongoing processes of discrimination, shifts in the prevailing economic climate, the development of a sophisticated racial ideology of "conservative egalitarianism" (or should we say "benign neglect"?)—in other words, all the concrete sociopolitical dynamics within which racial phenomena operate in the U.S.—are ignored in this approach. (p. 22)

It is important to note that the characterization of Asian Americans as model minorities who have overcome adversity to succeed supports the ethnicity-as-race paradigm.

Cultural-difference theorists such as Au and Jordan (1981), Erickson and Mohatt (1982), and Philips (1983) have demonstrated the significance that culture has on the educational experiences of students from culturally, ethnically, racially, and linguistically diverse backgrounds. In my critique of the ethnicity paradigm, I am not denying that culture influences the schooling experiences of students. I am, however, arguing that at Academic High the discourse of culture and ethnicity allowed the teachers and administrators to overlook structural barriers.

DENYING RACIAL TENSIONS

In addition to denying the existence of racial inequality, white teachers and administrators denied the existence of racial tension among Academic High students. According to Levine, Academic students were above the racial tensions that marked other city schools. During my first visit to Academic, Levine told me that interracial relations at his school were "good." To prove his point, Levine told me a story of how African American students at Academic had come to the assistance of their Asian peers. Levine reported that two years ago some Asian students from Academic were having problems at the subway station with African American students from other schools. Several times during his telling of this story, he stated that the African American students were "not from Academic, but from other schools." Furthermore, he suggested that the subways were always problem areas because students from other schools used the subways and that "there are often problems because a lot of kids from other schools are jealous of Academic students."

> Some Asian students reported having their gold necklaces snatched. We tried to advise our students not to wear their jewelry so that it shows, but . . . now, as an example of how well our kids get along . . . when this was all happening a group of our black students came into my office and offered to escort our Asian kids to the subways.

Levine provided this story as evidence of how Academic students lived together harmoniously. He was aware of the interracial tensions that marked the city and many of the public high schools, and his story was meant to illustrate the difference between students at Academic High and students at other schools. Levine suggested that students at Academic High were above interracial differences. He assumed that Academic High students were too smart to have prejudicial attitudes.

Levine's image of Academic as an oasis of interracial harmony was echoed by many white teachers during my early days at Academic. According to these teachers, there was little or no racial tension at Academic. In a city and in a school system marked by racial tension, these teachers painted Academic as being the exception. Teachers, students, and student teachers described AHS as a "model UN" where students of all races came together. Hal Tuverson, a gym teacher, said this to me:

> How do you like it here? Aren't the kids great? I just love 'em. This place is like the UN. Look out at the lunchroom . . . you don't see only whites with whites, and blacks with blacks, and Asians with Asians. Of course there's some of that, but our kids really mix here.

Although Mr. Tuverson maintained that students from different racial groups ate together, in my observations of the lunchroom, I found that integrated seating was the exception, not the rule. Yet Dr. Levine, Mr. Tuverson, and the other Academic High enthusiasts believed that Academic exemplified true social integration. Their image of AHS as the model UN denied the reality of racial segregation. In recording what these Academic aficionados said, I noted that they were all white.

Levine's image of Academic High as a peacefully integrated school did not prepare him for the outburst at the graduation exercises. His reaction was one of shock and anger. After the graduation, he told me repeatedly that he had almost "pulled the curtain" on the graduation exercises. After he calmed down, Levine began to see the event as an isolated incident. He suggested that parents and students from the south side were probably responsible for the outburst. He asserted that underqualified students from the south side had been accepted to Academic before his policies could take hold. He suggested that these students and their parents were ignorant and intolerant. In his words, "Before I came enrollment was down . . . they were taking anyone . . . warm bodies." Levine believed that there was a direct connection between tolerance and intelligence. He argued that this kind of outburst would never occur among the students admitted to the school under his system. Levine could not imagine that "smart kids" would be capable of racism.

Levine's beliefs concerning the connection between tolerance and intelligence were based on the belief that prejudice and racism are irrational. This view of racism argues that tolerance can be taught and that intolerance can be untaught. It assumes that racism is not in the best interest of those expressing the racism (Sleeter, 1993; Wellman, 1977). The belief that racism is based on ignorance denies the fact that racism has structural roots. It denies the fact that there might be rational/self-interested reasons to be racist. It denies the fact that attitudes toward others are influenced by relative status/position. Levine's vision of racism denied the fact that the school encouraged interracial competition and tension.

I would argue that the culture of competition at AHS promoted interracial tension. The competition to gain admission to the school created a zero-sum environment whereby groups perceived that a gain for another group necessarily meant a loss for their group. The sorting and tracking that took place upon walking through the school's front doors reminded students that not all are created equal and not all students were equally welcomed into the AHS community. The competition to gain insider status promoted hostility among groups on the periphery. Thus, Italian students from the south side who are shut out of the academic elite and other insider activities may in fact turn their hostility on Asian Americans who, they believe, are squeezing them out.

Like Mrs. Lewis, I would suggest that the extensive tracking system at AHS is redundant. Students have already demonstrated high standards in order to gain admission to the school. Additionally, I would argue that Academic's tradition of ranking students according to their cumulative grade-point average each year fuels unnecessary competition. Furthermore, the practice of posting the names of the ten top students in each class promotes the notion that only the students at the very top are winners.

While the policies/structures create an environment of competition among students, I would argue that the stereotyping of Asian Americans as model minorities sets Asian Americans up as the specific targets of jealousy. Asian Americans are used to blame the victims (i.e., African Americans) for their problems. Thus whiteness is erased, and people of color are left to fight among themselves. Asian Americans are used to support the claim that merit is neutral. Omi and Winant (1986) remind us, however, that merit is not neutral, but "it is a political construct, by which employers, schools, state agencies, etc. legitimate the allocation of benefits to favored groups (i.e., organized), constituencies, and deny the validity of competing claims" (p. 129). At Academic High, the fact that white students were well represented in the academic elite and the fact that white students dominated many of the high-status extracurricular activities were obscured by pointing to the success of Asian Americans. In short, Asian Americans were used as buffers between the African Americans and the whites at Academic High.

CHAPTER 5

Student Voices on Race

February 8, 1989—I ducked into the faculty cafeteria to grab a cup of tea during third lunch. As I was leaving, I ran right into Marsha, one of the student teachers, and we had a brief conversation about Academic. She mentioned that she thought the school was a little too competitive, but then she went on to say that she really liked being here because "there are kids from everywhere here." Furthermore, she asserted that all the kids got along with each other "just like a model UN." As I walked back into the student cafeteria, I scanned the room for familiar faces and I was struck by the irony of the UN metaphor. Much like it is in the real UN, people from different groups were all sitting in their separate corners.

This chapter analyzes the ways that white, African American, and Asian American students handle and interpret race relations at Academic High. I focus on how white students and African American students viewed Asian Americans. I argue that students' attitudes toward Asian Americans reflect their respective positions in the school. Negative attitudes toward Asian Americans were expressed by those who perceived Asians as a threat. Then, I focus on how students in the different Asian American identity groups viewed non-Asians and how they dealt with racism. The overarching questions in this chapter center on how the model minority stereotype, generally, and the conditions in the school, specifically, influenced race relations among the students.

WHITE STUDENTS

Like the white teachers at Academic High, most white students asserted that Academic High was a great school. They spoke proudly of the diversity of the student population and boasted that students of all races got along with each other. Dan McCarthy, a socially prominent "Edgewood type," described Academic High like this:

99

Academic is the best in the city. No doubt if I had to do it over
again, I'd do it again because there are people here from all over
the world. It's just the diversity here . . . I don't know if I'll ever
run into it again. Here is where I guess you can have your own
group—say it consists of Catholic or kids from your section of
the city—but when you get to the senior year it is your class that
brings you together.

Dan believed that students at Academic High struck a balance between
celebrating diversity and sharing a common identity as Academic High
students. Dan felt accepted at Academic High, and he assumed that students of all races felt equally at home at the school.

Dan McCarthy asserted that the fact that students "busted" on each
other was evidence of good interracial relations. Students defined "busting" as the practice of putting someone down or making jokes about
someone. "Busting" often took the form of derogatory comments regarding someone's race or ethnicity. In Dan's words:

In my advisory there's this ongoing thing—joke of where these
ethnic slurs go back and forth. . . . Some say that's bad, but as
one kid said, "If you can bust on someone, then you've sort of accepted them in a way." And it is that kind of backhanded way of
saying that you are one of us. It's like calling people nigger. With
Asians there are all these stereotypes, like they're all good in math
and go to MIT. I heard from Ken Wong that MIT means "made in
Taiwan." You can bust on yourself, and people can bust on you
without even a thought. We're all equal here.

Although I observed racial slurs being directed at Asian and African American students, I never witnessed racial slurs being directed at white students.
Busting was a unidirectional activity that left white students untouched.

Many African American and Asian American students reported that
they were offended by the racial busting, but most said that they rarely challenged the comments. Some tried to laugh the jokes off, and others reported
that the jokes actually hurt their feelings. The fact that most African Americans and Asian Americans did not challenge the busting indicates that they
accepted that whites were at the top of the social hierarchy inside and outside the school. Asian students and other students of color who were eager
to gain the acceptance of whites often colluded with whites in their racial
jokes about members of their own race. As noted earlier, some Korean-,
Asian-, and new wave–identified students referred to themselves as "chinks"
in order to make people laugh. John, a Korean-identified student, explained

that he busted on himself in order to put "Americans" at ease. Virginia Hsu, the Chinese American student who was selected to be the 1989 editor of the *Academic Blazer*, had a reputation for busting on Asians. Virginia asserted that she could not relate to any of the other Asian American students at Academic High and that she busted on Asians in order to make it clear that she was different from other Asians.

Adam Wilson, a socially prominent white student who was involved in sports and student government, reported that his two Korean American friends frequently made jokes about Asians:

> They refer to the Korean things as chink events. It seems almost derogatory, but at the same time, they go to them. It is offensive to me, but they say things like, "We just went to a chink party and it was decent." It's constant and I hear it all the time.

Although Adam reported being offended by the comments that his Korean friends made, he admitted that he occasionally laughed along with them. It is also important to note that Adam chose to socialize with these Asian American students and not with Asians who refused to participate in self-busting.

Humor, self-mockery, and clowning are self-protective and resistant strategies that racial minorities use to deal with the dominant group (Omi & Winant, 1986; Watkins, 1994). They are adaptations that the powerless group makes to deal with the powerful prior to the politicization of the powerless (Omi & Winant, 1986). One consequence of this strategy is that those in power often come to expect self-effacing behavior from racial minorities. In writing about Clarence Thomas, Toni Morrison (1992) notes that Thomas's habit of laughing at himself was a form of self-effacement that the white majority often demands of racial minorities.

At Academic High, Asian American students who refused to participate in self-busting were often accused of being humorless. Furthermore, many white students at Academic chose to befriend Asian American students who actively participated in self-busting. For example, Virginia Hsu's habit of making derogatory comments about Asians helped make her popular among her white peers. Karen Littlefield, one of Virginia's white friends from the *Blazer* staff, commented that she liked Virginia because she was not "snobby about being Chinese." Karen suggested that Asians who speak their native languages at school and who cannot take a joke about their ethnicity are "snobby." Similarly, Ken Wong's willingness to make jokes about his own race earned him Dan's laugh of approval. Dan appreciated Ken's joke about "MIT" because it fit into his stereotype that all Asians are good in math and science.

White Images of Asians

Most white students did not distinguish among the identity groups but saw all Asian Americans simply as Asians. The higher-achieving white students were, however, aware that the Korean students had a separate club. Like the majority of the white faculty, most white students described Asian Americans as hardworking students who excelled in math and science. In other words, they accepted the model minority stereotype of Asian Americans. Although most white students reported that they did not have any close friendships with Asian American students, they insisted that they respected their Asian American peers for their academic talent.

Asian American scholars writing on race have noted that white attitudes toward Asian Americans are influenced by white relationships with African Americans (Cho, 1993; Takagi, 1992). Writing about the portrayal of Korean Americans in the media, Cho (1993) writes:

> The embrace of the model minority myth by the media becomes a bear hug particularly at times when black-white tensions intensify and white America wishes to discipline African Americans. For example, Korean Americans were sympathetically represented during the racial tensions in New York following racist white violence and the African American deaths in Howard Beach and Bensonhurst. The boycott of Korean owned Family Red Apple grocery store in Brooklyn provided a welcome opportunity to discredit the African American community as "racist," linking the Red Apple boycott to the African American responses to Howard Beach and Bensonhurst. Other times Korean Americans will be sacrificed to communities of color to salve white conscience. (p. 204)

At Academic High white students' perspectives on Asian Americans were influenced by white relationships with African Americans and by their position relative to Asians. Academically and socially successful white students who were secure in their status held positive images regarding Asian Americans. These students were also sensitive to the critique of African American students who asserted that all was not well for them at Academic High. These white students responded to the African American students' challenge by holding Asian Americans up as exemplars of success. These students resisted any challenge to the model minority stereotype. According to the successful white students, Asian American "success" was proof of equal opportunity.

Jeff Pinsky, a Jewish student who was ranked in the top of the junior class, maintained that Asians were model minorities. Furthermore, he asserted that he could relate to Asians because they were like Jews. According to Jeff, Jews and Asians shared a common respect for education. In his words, "This sounds really weird, but I think that Asians are the Jews of this generation. And, I'm sort of a holdover. The values are a lot the same." Jeff attributed the academic success of Asians and Jews to their respective cultures, and he attributed the underachievement of other minorities to their respective cultures. Like many of the white teachers, Jeff equated race with ethnicity and culture. He believed that the "success" of Asian Americans and Jews proved that students from all races can achieve success if they have "good values." Jeff contrasted the "positive" stereotype of Asian Americans with the overtly negative stereotypes of African Americans and Latinos. He noted that although stereotypes were often inaccurate, he had noticed that many African Americans did experience academic difficulties. Jeff interpreted the situation at Academic High as confirmation that Asians were good students and that other minorities did not care about education.

The one group of white students who expressed direct hostility toward Asian Americans were the students who hung out on the east lawn of the school. The east lawn was dominated by working-class Italian Americans from the south side. The South-side Italians, as they are known, have strong connections to their neighborhood, and their attitudes toward racial minorities have been influenced by the racial tensions in the south side of the city. Although the south side of the city is known as a working-class, Italian American neighborhood, it is also home to working-class and poor African Americans and Southeast Asian refugees. The south side has been marked by racial tension among its Asian, African American, and white residents. East Lawners referred to the Asian Americans as "chinks and gooks" and referred to the Asian American Studies course as "gook studies." According to my Asian American informants, East Lawners regularly sat on the steps to the east entrance and hurled invectives at Asian students passing by their turf. On one occasion, while I was walking with a group of Asian students, I witnessed and experienced this behavior. In classes, these students often imitated Asian accents and ridiculed Asian names. The East Lawners challenged the Asian students' right to be in the United States and often suggested that they "go back to where [they] came from."

Racism among the white working class has been identified by many who study the working class (Weis, 1990; Willis, 1977). In discussing white, working-class anger toward Asians, L. M. Wong (1993) has argued that the white working class see Asians as a threat to whiteness itself:

> The white working class, positioned at a critical juncture, is manipulated into racism but most often, these murderous acts are committed not just because of their class interests, but they come to think of themselves and their interests as the embodiments and protectors of whiteness. (p. 33)

The East Lawners saw Asian Americans as foreigners who were invading their school, their neighborhoods, and their country. They feared that Asian Americans were taking the place of whites at Academic High, and they believed that it was necessary to protect their turf from the invasion of Asians. East Lawners were very critical of the ASA, KSA, and the BSU, and some argued that since Asians and African Americans have their own clubs that white students should be allowed to establish a club for white students.

Although the south-side Italians who socialized on the east lawn were white, it is important to remember that they were not well represented in the academic elite or in any of the more academically prestigious groups (e.g., *Academic Blazer*) that would make them insiders at Academic High. In fact, south-side Italians were outsiders within the white population. The outsider status of south-side Italian Americans was conspicuously apparent when Levine suggested that they were probably responsible for the outburst at graduation. The zero-sum atmosphere at Academic High encouraged competition among students who were outsiders. Students who were outsiders at Academic High tried to elevate themselves by attacking groups whom they perceived to be less powerful. Thus the students from the south side vented their frustrations over their outsider status on Asian Americans.

The one south-sider who agreed to an interview with me was Lisa Rossini. The Rossini family had lived on the south side of the city for generations, and in that sense Lisa was a south-sider, but at AHS her membership in the MG program distinguished her from the other south-siders. Lisa spent most of her free time in the social science MG room. She was an insider in the world of the high achievers and did not spend any time with the East Lawners. Unlike other south-siders, Lisa did not express any hostility toward Asian Americans. Lisa's attitude toward Asian Americans was based on her status within the school. As an academic insider, Lisa did not feel threatened by Asian Americans. She reported that although she did not really know any Asian Americans personally, she knew that they "do well in school." Like other high achievers, Lisa reported that she respected Asian Americans for being smart. Her attitude toward Asian Americans demonstrates how attitudes toward others are influenced by status and position. At Academic High, Lisa gained status through her identity as a high-achieving student in the top academic tracks.

AFRICAN AMERICAN STUDENTS

Unlike white students, African American students described Academic High as a far cry from utopia. Contrary to the integrated image that many white students spoke about, African American students described

Academic as a segregated school. Jackie Brown, the president of the Black Student Union, described the race relations at Academic like this: "Everyone gets along, but nobody mixes." She also asserted that white students were at the top of the social hierarchy.

African American students were particularly concerned with the underrepresentation of African American students in the top ranks and academic tracks. African American students repeatedly pointed out that African American students were not only underrepresented in the upper tracks and higher ranks but also were the most likely group of students to drop out or fail out of Academic High. Beverly Watkins, a high-achieving African American student who was headed for Wesleyan College in the fall of 1989, put it like this: "It's a phenomenon that few blacks are in the star and AP classes." For those African Americans in the top tracks, their social experience was often difficult. Mrs. Lewis noted that "black students in AP and star classes often aren't liked [by other black students]." Keesha Fox (introduced in Chapter 4), another African American student in the top tracks, spoke about the pressure of being one of the few African American students in honors and AP courses:

> I know I feel pressure because there are few African American students in those classes. The pressure comes from representing the African American person. People [non-African Americans] look at me not like Keesha, but Keesha the black girl. And with hanging out with all those whites in my classes, African Americans called me an Oreo. You know, they'd say I wanted to be white.

Keesha's experience is reminiscent of the experiences of high-achieving African American students in Fordham's (1991) study who are accused of "acting white."

African American Student Images of Asians

Like the white students, most African American students did not distinguish among the Asian American identity groups. African American students often used the terms *Asian*, *Chinese*, and *Korean* interchangeably. Most African American students stereotyped Asian American students as math and science geniuses. According to many African American students, Asian Americans were highly successful students who were garnering more than their share of the academic accolades. Although white students were well represented in the upper ranks and in the higher tracks, the majority of African American students concentrated their criticism on what they perceived to be the overrepresentation of Asians in the academic elite.

Within the racist discourse, there is a silence surrounding whiteness (Dyer, 1993; Frankenberg, 1993; Roman, 1993). This silence normalizes whiteness and naturalizes white power and privilege.

> Power in contemporary society habitually passes itself off as embodied in the normal as opposed to the superior (cf. Marcuse, 1964). This is common to all forms of power, but it works in a peculiarly seductive way with whiteness, because of the way it seems rooted, in commonsense thought, in things other than ethnic difference. The very terms we used to describe the major ethnic divide presented by western society, "black" and "white," are imported from and naturalized by other discourses. (Dyer, 1993, p. 142)

The model minority stereotype serves to reinforce the racial order by focusing on Asian American success and redirecting attention away from whites. Thus I would argue that the African American students' failure to challenge white success is related to the silence that surrounds whiteness in general.

Because of the comparative and competitive nature of the model minority stereotype of Asian Americans, many African Americans saw Asian Americans as a threat. According to Keesha Fox, "there's a stereotype of Asians being superbrains and there is some resentment." Arthur Jackson, an African American student active in the BSU, made this comment regarding Asian American student success: "A lot of people I know don't like Asian people because they are intimidated by their intelligence. They say, 'they came over here and they bought up everything and now look at them in school.'" Arthur's friends believed that Asian Americans get rich by buying up businesses in African American neighborhoods. They believed that Asian American success had been achieved at the expense of African Americans. In this way, the stereotype of Asian Americans as high achievers becomes blurred with the stereotype that Asian Americans are economic threats. In writing about the aftermath of the first Rodney King decision, Cho (1993) argued that the fact that Asians are stereotyped as callous economic competitors and model minorities contributed to the fact that Korean merchants were targeted by looters. African American students interpreted Asian American student success at Academic High as confirmation of their fear that Asian Americans were taking over. According to Arthur's friends, Asian American success inside and outside school was a threat.

African American student anger at Asian Americans came out in the form of insults and accusations. On several occasions I observed African American students imitating Asian accents and ridiculing Asian names. During moments of anger, African Americans would tell Asians to "go back to where you came from." Like the East Lawners, many African

American students accused Asian Americans of being foreigners who did not have the same rights as "real" Americans. In writing about the tensions between African Americans and Korean merchants, Jo (1992) argues that African Americans are angry at what they perceive to be the fast social mobility of Asians in the face of continued black oppression.

> For many years, blacks have heard about the success of Asian Americans. Compared with blacks, they seem to have few problems with assimilation. Their putative economic success is the key indicator of their assimilation into the mainstream. (p. 405)

African American students at Academic were angry about what they perceived to be the quick success of Asian Americans. They saw Asian Americans as yet another group who had climbed over African Americans on their road to success.

Although the tension between African Americans and Asian Americans begins outside Academic High, the conditions inside Academic High contribute to the continued tension between the groups. While white students were positioned as the insiders, Asian American and African American students were positioned as the outsiders who were trying to gain insider status. Within the hierarchical culture of the institution, academic achievement is the most important way outsiders can gain insider status. Thus Asian students who were academically successful were able to gain insider status in the world of academia. Furthermore, the faculty and staff flaunted Asian American success at African Americans. In other words, they used Asian American success to silence the inequality experienced by African Americans and to defend the status quo. Given that the model minority stereotype pits Asian Americans against African Americans, African Americans believed that a gain for Asians meant a loss for them. Mr. Fox's comment about "Asians taking the place of blacks" at Academic reflects this underlying competition. The academic problems experienced by African American male students reminded African Americans at Academic High of the problems faced by African American males in the larger society.

In contrast to the majority of African American students, African American students who had gained status either as high academic achievers or as leaders in student government argued that white racism prevented African Americans from achieving equality. One such student, Jackie Brown, asserted that many white teachers at Academic High made African Americans feel unwelcome. In her words, "teachers have this image that this is a place where good Jewish boys go." High-achieving African American students were critical of what they perceived to be the overrepresentation of whites in the top ranks. These students spoke to me of the need for greater understanding between African Americans and Asians. During the 1987 school year, progressive leaders in the ASA and in the BSU who were interested in improved relations between African Americans and Asians organized a workshop that focused on interracial relations between African Americans and Asian Americans. Jackie, the 1988-89 BSU president, remembered the workshop as one of the few times that Asian Americans and African Americans got together and spoke honestly about their feelings regarding each other. She explained that while Asian Americans and African Americans held stereotypic ideas about each other, the workshop helped students to work beyond the stereotypes. Jackie maintained that more workshops were needed. The attitudes that the high-achieving African American students have toward Asians suggest that the relationships between African Americans and Asians are rooted in material conditions. That is, when African Americans and Asian Americans are not in direct competition for resources, they have little reason to be hostile toward each other.

ASIAN AMERICAN STUDENTS

Asian American students at Academic High understood that whites were seated at the top of the U.S. racial hierarchy. Most Asian American students embraced the model minority image of Asian Americans and used it to elevate themselves above other racial minorities. In addition to accepting the model minority stereotype, most Asian American students accepted the concomitant stereotype that African Americans are lazy and inferior. In this section, I examine how Asian American students in the four identity groups negotiated interracial relations. I also return to the issue of how members of the four Asian American identity groups responded to racism.

Korean-Identified Students

As discussed previously, Korean-identified students looked up to their white, middle-class peers and made attempts to get closer to them. These students argued that they deserved to be closer to whites because they were better than other minorities. In contrast to their attitudes toward whites, Korean-identified students looked down on their African American peers and made attempts to distance themselves from them. These students held blatantly negative stereotypes about African Americans. They asserted that African Americans were uneducated and that they were lazy welfare cheats. It is interesting to note that they held similar stereotypes of Southeast Asians.

During a group interview with Korean-identified students, I asked them to describe Korean relations with African Americans. Initially they seemed hesitant to answer my question, but eventually Brian Sung said, "OK, for instance . . . an example, if a white person, a friend, bought a soda, we drink it around. But, if a black person . . . if they bought a soda we never do, we might think they have AIDS or something." Brian's peers all nodded in agreement. They associated African Americans with disease, poverty, and crime.

During another conversation, Korean-identified students asserted that the presence of African American residents threatened a "good neighborhood." When I asked Korean-identified students where they got their attitudes about African Americans, they spoke about the "rowdy" behavior of African Americans, and they began to recite the problems between African Americans and Korean Americans in the city. Although they complained about tensions between African Americans and Korean Americans, they did not mention the fact that there had also been problems between whites and Korean Americans in the city. When I attempted to get them to talk about the problems between Korean Americans and whites, they responded by redirecting the conversation back to African American–Korean American tensions.

Korean-identified students' attitudes toward whites and African Americans were influenced by their desire to move ahead socially and economically. As discussed in Chapter 2, Korean parents believed that "learning American ways" (i.e., white, middle-class ways) was essential to success. They wanted their children to socialize with other Koreans in order to maintain a Korean identity and to socialize with white, middle-class Americans in order to gain status. They also wanted their children to stay away from African Americans because they feared that contact with African Americans might hurt their status. In writing about the relationship between Korean merchants and African Americans, Jo (1992) argues that concern with status leads Korean merchants to distance themselves from African Americans:

> Korean merchants in the black community witness unemployed Blacks in dilapidated surroundings and observe a black work ethic far different from their own. Some of these merchants begin to question their ability to achieve their hopes and aspirations, and recoil at the thought of becoming one of "them." To many Koreans, the quality of the black life-style not only reinforces their earlier stereotype that Blacks are "lazy and dumb," but also serves as a warning that a close association in whatever form with Blacks may cause these merchants to fail. The more Koreans think that their goals and sense of a better future conflict with the values and ideals of poor inner-city Blacks, the more they want to distance themselves from the Blacks in case they be permanently identified with Blacks. (p. 406)

Although it was not clear to me whether Korean parents formed their opinions regarding race in the United States or in Korea, Cho (1993) argues that Korean attitudes toward African Americans are formed prior to coming to the United States by western media and western military influence. I would argue that the model minority stereotype negatively affects Koreans' attitudes toward African Americans. The model minority stereotype implicitly stereotypes African Americans as a lazy group of people who fail to help themselves. I would add that the position of African Americans inside Academic High confirmed Korean-identified students' belief that African Americans were inferior.

Korean-identified students believed that any racism they faced on the part of whites was temporary. They believed that if they dressed and spoke like their white, middle-class peers and otherwise acted like white, middle-class people, they would eventually be accepted. Korean-identified students were aware that they were stereotyped as model minorities, and they believed that this was proof that Koreans were superior to other minorities (e.g., African Americans). They also believed that if they proved themselves to be model minorities, they could earn the respect of white Americans and move up the social ladder. As noted earlier, the desire to live up to the model minority standards led Korean-identified students to deny the existence of academic problems among Korean students. The Korean-identified students' response to racism is not unlike the response of other immigrant groups who choose to overlook their experiences with white racism (Gibson, 1988; Ogbu, 1987).

Despite the fact that Korean-identified students talked about having white friends, most of them socialized solely with other Koreans. Of my twenty-three Korean-identified student informants, only five had white friends with whom they socialized regularly. Out of these five students, one was a Korean girl who had been adopted by a white family when she was a young child. This student did not socialize with Korean-identified students or with other Asian Americans, but socialized exclusively with white students. Because she had been adopted and raised by a white, middle-class family, her Korean peers considered her to be almost white and therefore outside their circle.

The one friendship between a white student and a Korean-identified student that I observed regularly was the relationship between Kay Rowe and Karen Littlefield. Kay and Karen were both members of the *Academic Blazer*. Additionally, they were both in the school orchestra and both in the top academic track. Kay successfully achieved the Korean style of a dual identity. She was active in the KSA and in non-Korean activities. Her negotiation of the two worlds, however, came at a personal cost. Karen described Kay's situation like this:

> Kay is in the middle . . . I mean, sometimes she has conflicts with both groups. It's a struggle for her, but. . . . She's had a lot of parties for the Korean club, and she would invite us [white friends] and say like, "you could come if you like. . . ." But of course we wouldn't come. First of all, we wouldn't understand a word that was being said. It would not be a good situation.

Although Kay had Korean and white friends, she was often on the outside of both worlds. Many of her white peers did not understand her ties to the Korean community, and ironically, her Korean-identified peers criticized her for achieving the very success with whites that they advocated.

Asian-Identified Students

Students who identified as Asian were generally reserved in regard to discussions of race. As noted in Chapter 2, these students generally socialized solely with other Asians. The fact that Asian-identified students reserved the term *American* for white people was my first clue regarding how these students understood the racial dynamics in the United States. Although Asian-identified students referred to all white people as "Americans," they referred to nonwhites by their specific race. Asian-identified students joked that Americans were all blond-haired and blue-eyed.

My second significant piece of data concerning how these Asian-identified students viewed non-Asians was the fact that many of them used a derogatory Cantonese term for black people. The first time I heard students use the term was when I was on the bus with a group of Asian-identified students on the way to a sporting event and we drove through a predominately African American neighborhood. Many of the students who used the term were not Cantonese speakers, and I was surprised to hear the term. The students began to make nasty comments about the neighborhood, and I heard them use the Cantonese term for blacks. When I questioned the students regarding their use of the term, they explained that "all Asians use the word" so that they can talk about African American people without being understood. Asian-identified students blamed African Americans for high crime rates and violence against Asians. All of the Asian-identified students told me that their parents would be strongly opposed to their having an intimate relationship with an African American person.

A common complaint among Asian-identified students was that African Americans got a "free ride" in the United States. The high-achieving, Asian-identified students were the most vociferously critical of African Americans. Thai Le (discussed in Chapter 3), for example, was adamantly against affirmative action because he believed it unfairly advantages

African Americans and Latinos and disadvantages Asians. The following is an excerpt from an interview with Thai in which we discussed the controversy surrounding Asian American admissions in higher education:

> *Thai*: I hate it [quotas]. Because I think it should be based on ability. This is why I hate quotas—if you're black and you're female you could get into Harvard anytime you want. That's the way it is. Because they want to have a certain number of blacks. They want to have a certain number of Hispanics.
>
> *SL*: Do you really believe this? Anyway, who's responsible for setting quotas or deciding who gets in?
>
> *Thai*: I think the different groups. Like there's a black community who look out for black rights.
>
> *SL*: But who is in power? Who makes the decisions regarding admissions?
>
> *Thai*: Colleges?
>
> *SL:* Yeah! And who controls the colleges? The black community?
>
> *Thai*: But I'm talking about standards.
>
> *SL*: Who sets the standards?

Thai understood that I was challenging his ideas, but he was convinced of his own opinions. I would argue that Thai needed to believe in the meritocratic system in order to participate in it. He and other Asian-identified students with self-proclaimed neoconservative politics believed in the fairness of the meritocratic system and believed that their own success was the evidence that supported their opinions. Thai told me that he had learned all about the quotas against Asians in the newspapers and in magazines such as *Time*. I would also assert that his encounter with Mr. Edwards about the minority scholarship banquet (described in Chapter 4) confirmed his opinions about his African American peers.

Although Asian-identified students saw white people as the dominant group and respected that status, they maintained their distance from them. For example, Jeff Pinsky was admired by the high-achieving, Asian-identified students for his academic prowess. Many of the high achievers referred to Jeff as "Dr. Pinsky." Jeff tried to establish co-membership with Asian students by pointing to what he saw as the similarities between Jews and Asians. Despite Jeff's desire to form close friendships with the high-achieving Asians, the Asian-identified students never thought of Jeff as part of their group. According to the Asians, the only thing they shared in common with Jeff was high academic achievement. They suggested that Jeff could not understand "Asian things." Asian-identified students believed that discrimination joined Asians together.

Asian-identified students were aware that they faced barriers due to their ethnicity/race, but they seemed to attribute their problems to cultural differences or language barriers. Some Asian-identified students blamed themselves for the racism they faced. These students internalized the negative images of Asian Americans and the positive images of whites. For example, they internalized the racist standards that marked Asian accents as bad. Another Asian-identified student explained what he thought Asian students should do to gain the acceptance of whites:

> First of all they [Asians] don't speak English right. And second of all you dress up different. And you don't listen to punk rock or any American music. So, obviously they start to treat you different because you act different. I'm not trying to say that you should change yourself to completely American and become part of them. I mean, what I believe is that you should pick up the good of a different culture. Then when people see you, they will accept you.

This student, like many Asian- and Korean-identified students, rationalized experiences with racism. This student believed that Asians would gain acceptance once they overcame language barriers and adopted white American styles. As pointed out in Chapter 3, Thai Le believed that because of his Asian accent he could not be a lawyer. Although Thai is probably correct in his assumption that his accent might limit his success as a lawyer, it is significant that he has chosen not to fight the racism that marks his accent as inferior. I would argue that his decision not to fight this racism is based on his understanding of his social position. In other words, he understands that as a relative newcomer to the United States he does not have a great deal of power.

Like their Korean-identified peers, Asian-identified students were encouraged by their parents to work hard and ignore students who made derogatory comments regarding their ethnicity/race. According to Ogbu (1987, 1991), this attitude toward discrimination is typical of immigrant minorities. In regard to immigrant minorities, Ogbu (1991) writes: "They rationalize the prejudice and discrimination by saying as 'guests' in a foreign land they have no choice but to tolerate prejudice and discrimination" (p. 21). Asian- and Korean-identified students accepted that they were outsiders in the United States, and they understood that within the racial hierarchy they were beneath whites. Many blamed themselves for the discrimination they faced. They did not expect the dominant group to accommodate them but believed that they needed to make accommodations in order to gain acceptance. Asian- and Korean-identified students did not speak about institutional or structural barriers.

New Wavers

Like the Asian-identified students, the new wave–identified students had little to do with non-Asians. Although new wavers generally stayed out of the way of their white peers, they took a confrontational approach to their relations with their African American peers. Of the four identity groups, the Asian new wavers were the most blatantly racist against African Americans. Dorothy Chin, the 1988–89 president of the ASA, and also one of the most popular new wave girls, said this when describing what her new wave friends thought about African Americans:

> All of them don't like blacks as much because I think everybody
> has had a bad experience with blacks. . . . When you live in the
> city, they are so wild and they are so . . . well, by the way they act
> you wouldn't want them in your house.

Like the Asian- and Korean-identified students, the new wavers held stereotypes about African Americans being "lazy, uneducated welfare cheats."

While Korean- and Asian-identified students tried to prove themselves superior to African Americans while maintaining their distance from African Americans, new wavers competed directly with African Americans. As noted earlier, African American students expressed their anger toward Asian Americans through verbal taunts. While Korean- and Asian-identified students chose to ignore these comments, new wavers chose to respond with their own set of insults. The new wavers' competitive and contemptuous attitude toward African Americans was expressed by Lan:

> Sometime I still walk home or walk somewhere they [blacks]
> would call you chink and stuff. Call you not American . . . should
> go back and stuff. I tell them, "you not American neither . . . you
> ship came off America. You have no right to talk to us like that." I
> tell them to go back to Africa . . . "you have no right to talk to us
> like that. This is a free country. You were brought over like slaves
> . . . we better off than that."

Lan and her new wave friends were unwilling to sit back and take insults from African American students. Lan's comments reflected her understanding that African Americans were below whites in the racial hierarchy. New wavers accepted that whites were at the top of the racial hierarchy, but they refused to be on the bottom. Thus Lan and other new wavers put down other minority groups in order to elevate their own group. The potential for conflict between two groups is greatest when the groups think they are superior to each other. Edward Chang writes, "When the perceived or real power of two groups is equal, or if each group believes that it is superior over the other group, there is high probability for violent and direct confrontation" (quoted in J. Chang, 1993, p. 102).

New wavers' attitudes regarding African Americans are influenced by Asian American and African American tension in the city. Most of the new wavers lived in neighborhoods with African American people, and most were also in the same academic tracks as their African American peers. In short, new wavers and African Americans competed over the same turf at home and at school. New wave attitudes toward African Americans were also influenced by their relations with their Asian American peers. As noted earlier, Korean- and Asian-identified students maligned new wavers. Korean-identified students accused new wavers of being "tacky," and high-achieving, Asian-identified students denigrated new wavers for being low achievers and troublemakers. In the eyes of the Korean- and Asian-identified students, new wave students were just slightly better than African Americans. New wavers were aware of how the Korean- and Asian-identified students viewed them and responded by trying to prove that they were better than African Americans.

While the new wavers were vociferous in their complaints about African Americans, they rarely mentioned whites. When I asked Dorothy about whites, she hesitated and then replied that "I never think about them." After I persisted, Dorothy described white people she has known who are "really rich" or "really well educated." Like Korean- and Asian-identified students, she referred to whites as "Americans" and to all other groups by their specific races. Although few new wavers had close contacts with middle-class whites, I would argue that new wavers were well aware of the status of whites in society. Freire (1986) has written that subordinate groups are always knowledgeable about groups in power because that knowledge is crucial for survival.

New wave students understood that whites stereotyped Asian as "academic nerds," and they believed that this stereotype limited their social acceptance among non-Asians. I would argue that new wavers' resistance to school was their attempt to rid themselves of the nerd image. Lan said, "I see my friends, some they act so dumb . . . so not be like a nerd." Lan asserted that cutting class and smoking were two ways in which new wavers tried to be "more American—more cool." I would add that new wavers co-opted aspects of black urban youth culture in their efforts to avoid being cast as Asian nerds. I observed new wavers using black urban slang such as "posse" and "homeboy," and I also noted that new wavers imitated the way that African American students danced. In his study of

Vietnamese American high school students, Centri (1993) found a similar pattern. As in my study, Centri's informants denigrated African Americans but also tried to emulate black style. I would argue that new wavers imitated black popular culture because they viewed it as having a high level of "cool capital," which Asian Americans lacked. Thus, despite their negative attitudes toward African Americans, new wavers imitated black urban youth culture.

Asian American–Identified Students

Asian American–identified students were articulate critics of racism. They argued that white people held the power in the United States and were the beneficiaries of racism. As noted earlier, Asian American–identified students criticized the model minority stereotype for being a tool of white racism. They argued that the model minority stereotype was inaccurate and that it fueled tension between Asian Americans and other minorities. Asian American–identified students asserted that black–Asian tension at Academic High was promoted by the extensive tracking and ranking system, including posting the names of the top ten students, and by teachers' stereotypes of Asians as model minorities.

Of all the identity groups, Asian American–identified students were the only ones to challenge the status of whites. As already discussed, Korean-, Asian-, and new wave–identified students accepted the dominance of whites in the social hierarchy. They accepted the unspoken rule that whites represented the norm of U.S. society and that all others represented deviations from this norm. The fact that Korean-, Asian-, and new wave–identified students believed that whites were the only "real Americans" is an example of their acceptance of the whiteness norm. As Frankenberg (1993) reminds us, however, whites are "raced" and their position in the racial hierarchy is constructed. In other words, race shapes the lives of white people in addition to the lives of people of color (Frankenberg, 1993; Roman, 1993). The fact that whiteness is the norm in the United States represents one of the greatest forms of entitlement that whites experience (McLaren, 1991; Sleeter, 1993). Failure to question the notion of whiteness as the norm allows white racial dominance to continue. One example of how Asian American–identified students questioned white norms was by their calling attention to the fact that Native Americans were the original Americans.

Despite the fact that Asian American–identified students were the most critical of white racism, they were also the group who had the most direct interpersonal contact with white people. For example, Xuan Nguyen, the most outspoken Asian American student, was the student most frequently named by white students as a leader in the Asian American student community. Xuan and other Asian American–identified students often socialized with white students they described as "politically progressive." Since most Asian American–identified students had been in the United States since they were very young, they were accustomed to interacting with whites. Unlike Korean- and Asian-identified students, the Asian American–identified students were not seeking white approval or acceptance. They have already achieved what Korean- and Asian-identified students hope to achieve. I would argue that the Asian American–identified students' relationships with white students allowed them to be more critical of whites.

The experience of Young Hun Pak, a Korean student who identified as Asian American, illustrates how "being accepted" by whites can influence a student's interpretation of racism. Young came to the United States in 1979 and settled with her family in a medium-sized town in Pennsylvania. As one of the only Asian American children in the town, Young learned "American" ways quickly. Young reported that during her time in this town, she became more comfortable with whites than with Asian Americans. In her words:

> I used to think I was white. I wanted to be white. This was when I lived in a small town. No one discriminated against me there— not in an overt way. I had white friends. Then in fourth grade, I moved here. I saw that Asians were treated like the scum of the earth. I thought that wasn't going to happen to me. I don't have an accent. I have white friends. But I walked around and people called me chink. They called me chink to my face.

For Young, these first experiences with overt racism came as a real shock. Before these experiences, she had believed that she was different from other Asians. She believed that she would be able to distance herself from other Asian Americans because she could "fit in" with white people. Like Asian- and Korean-identified students, Young had believed that speaking English without an accent and knowing "American culture" could protect her from racism. Young stated that her experiences in the city have taught her that friendships with white people and efforts at assimilation cannot protect her from racism.

Asian American–identified students believed that Asian Americans need "Asian only" spaces where they can talk honestly about their experiences as Asian Americans without worrying what non-Asians think or feel. For example, they were frustrated by the presence of non-Asians at ASA meetings. Asian American–identified students also believed Asian

Americans should learn about their own history. These students worked with Ms. Campbell, an African American teacher in the social science department, to develop the Asian American Studies course at Academic High. Although the Asian American–identified students supported the course, the Asian-, Korean-, and new wave–identified students were not interested in taking the course.

Asian American–identified students argued that Asian Americans, African Americans, Latinos, and Native Americans share a common experience as racial minorities in the United States. Based on this understanding, Asian American–identified students contended that Asian American students should forge closer relations with African American students. Asian American–identified students had worked with leaders in the BSU to sponsor the previous year's workshop on black and Asian relations. They noted that similar workshops were necessary if African Americans and Asians were to overcome their differences.

INTERRACIAL ANIMOSITY, COEXISTENCE, AND FRIENDSHIP

Contrary to the white teachers' image of Academic High as a model UN where students of all races get along, my data suggest that Academic High was racially factionalized. Based on observations and interviews with students, I would argue that the interracial situation at Academic High might best be described as one of peaceful coexistence. Despite the appearance of racial harmony, interracial tension between African Americans and Asian Americans and between Asian Americans and white, working-class students lay beneath the surface. Although there were not any incidents of interracial violence during the time I was at Academic, there was little in the way of interracial socializing. Students spoke to each other in classes, but interracial friendships were the exception.

When interracial friendships did exist, they were more likely to exist between a white student and a minority student than between two minority students. For example, out of the 82 Asian American students (Korean-identified and all other Asian Americans) with whom I had some regular contact, 21 of these students had at least a casual friendship (limited to school hours) with at least one white student. By contrast, only three of these students had friendships with at least one African American student. Given the racial hierarchy at Academic, I would assert that minority students viewed friendships with white students as a status symbol. Thus friendship with white students was a way to gain access to insider status.

Despite the fact that there were not many friendships between African Americans and Asian Americans, one of the more notable cross-racial friendships within the academic elite was between a Taiwanese American student and an African American student. Mei Mei and Charmaine were in the same math and science classes; according to both Charmaine and Mei Mei, they were friends. Although Mei Mei spent most of her free time with Asian Americans and Charmaine with African Americans, they liked and respected each other. For example, although they each sat with their own cliques at the junior prom (Mei Mei with Asian Americans and Charmaine with African Americans), they were careful to find each other during the evening in order to chat and share a fast dance.

Another friendship between an African American student and an Asian American student developed on a sports team. Donna, an African American/Puerto Rican student, and Jin, a Chinese American student, were doubles partners on the girls' badminton team. Donna and Jin chose to be doubles partners for three consecutive years. Their friendship included conversations about school, family, and dating. The relationship between Mei Mei and Charmaine and that between Donna and Jin suggest that friendships between Asian Americans and African Americans can develop when the students do not see their groups as competing.

Although interracial tensions between African American and Asian American students as well as between Asian American and white, working-class students were influenced by conditions outside the school, I would maintain that the school aggravated these tensions. Academic High School influenced interracial relations through the system of tracking and through the perpetuation of the model minority stereotype of Asian Americans. The fact that few African American students were in the top tracks served to confirm Asian American students' ideas that African Americans were inferior students. On the other hand, African American students interpreted the situation at Academic High as confirmation that African Americans were once again being excluded and that Asians were "taking over."

CHAPTER 6

Reflecting Again
on the Model Minority

The Asian American students at Academic High School clearly demonstrate that there is no single Asian American experience, identity, or perspective. While some of the students embraced the achievement ideology and expressed pro-school attitudes and behaviors, others were ambivalent about the role of school in their lives. While some of the students achieved model minority success and were headed for elite universities, others struggled to pass their classes. Asian American students had varied understandings of race and racism, different types of relationships with non-Asians, and different responses to the model minority stereotype. The diversity among Asian American students at AHS represents but a small fraction of the diversity among Asian Americans in the larger society.

Despite the many differences among Asian American youth at Academic High, all of the Asian American students were affected by the stereotype that Asian Americans are high-achieving model minorities. Teachers and non-Asian students generally assumed that all Asian Americans were high-achieving model minorities, an assumption that negatively affected students who failed to live up to the standards of the stereotype. As a hegemonic construct, the model minority stereotype served as a wedge between Asian Americans and other groups of people of color, and shaped the way all Asian American students viewed themselves. The school district categorized all East and Southeast Asian students at Academic High as "Asian" regardless of whether or not students embraced a pan-ethnic identity. Similarly, at Academic High most teachers and students viewed all students of East and Southeast Asian descent as being "Asian," thereby erasing significant differences. In short, all of the Chinese, Korean, Vietnamese, Lao, and Cambodian students at AHS had to contend with both the pan-ethnic category of "Asian" and the model minority stereotype.

Asian American students from all four identity groups were aware that non-Asians lumped all Asian Americans into one category, and stereotyped Asian Americans as model minorities. Students were also aware that Asians are a racialized minority group—that is, compared to other groups.

The process of identity formation among all of the Asian American students was influenced by their perceptions regarding their positions and locations within society and their understanding of their interests. Asian American students in all four groups judged their situations by comparing their social positions to that of whites, nonwhite minorities, and other Asian Americans. Significantly, the four identity groups came to different conclusions about their positions in the larger society and different conclusions about how they should respond to dominant society. Some Asian American youth gladly accepted the model minority label, others struggled to live up to it, and still others were critical of it. While most embraced a pan-ethnic identity they applied varied and diverse meanings to being Asian. Asian American–identified students, for example, viewed pan-ethnic identification as an overtly political act, but Asian-identified students were more interested in the social support they gained from socializing with others who shared a similar culture and similar social positions.

In this revised conclusion to the book, I will revisit the four identity groups in light of the recent research on immigrant education, and the literature on Asian Americans in particular. Although the students in my study are unique individuals who attended a particular school at a specific moment in history, the students in the four identity groups represent general types of Asian American students who are present in our schools today. Although youth styles have changed, and the names of student categories may vary, a review of the literature on Asian Americans suggests that we can still find students who reflect these general categories today. Furthermore, I will argue that Asian American students continue to face many similar issues in the early 21st century. I will conclude the book by taking a final opportunity to reflect on the role of the model minority stereotype within the context of AHS and within the larger society.

ASIAN AMERICAN IDENTITIES REVISITED

Korean-Identified Students

As I argued throughout the book, the vast majority of Korean American students at Academic High identified solely as Korean. That is, they rejected a pan-ethnic identity as Asian, and worked hard to distinguish themselves from other Asian Americans at the school. As noted in Chapter 2, Korean-identified students were exceptionally critical of new wave students because they saw the new wavers' underachievement and poverty as threats to the model minority image of Asians, which they attempted to achieve. Within the larger Asian American student community

Korean-identified students were seen as different and separate from other Asian Americans. As the group who bore the brunt of the Korean-identified students' criticism, new wave students were particularly quick to assert that Korean-identified students were elitist and ethnocentric. Similarly, in her study on low-income Southeast Asian youth Reyes (2007) found that many of her research participants "accused Korean Americans of having superiority complexes and of refusing to mingle with other Asian American ethnic groups" (p. 124).

The Korean identity expressed by most Korean American students at Academic High was one promoted by their parents and by the larger Korean immigrant community in the area. Other researchers have identified this strong ethnic solidarity that I observed among Korean American students as well (Kibria, 2002; Lew, 2006; Min, 1998). The literature on ethnic identity is roughly divided between those who argue that ethnic groups are "communities of culture" and those who argue that ethnic groups are "communities of interest" (Espiritu, 1992). Among Korean-identified students at AHS, ethnic identity appears to be both about culture/heritage and interest. Kibria (2002) found that within Korean immigrant families, parents emphasized primordial conceptions of Korean ethnicity that emphasized blood and common ancestry. Although I never heard a Korean-identified student speak about his or her ethnicity in these specific terms, many spoke of their Korean ethnicity as a given and as something that defined them in an essential kind of way. Indeed, the cultural and linguistic homogeneity among Korean immigrants supports in-group cohesion, and understandings of Korean ethnicity as essential (Min, 1991). Researchers have also suggested that the strong ethnic solidarity among Korean immigrants is a protective reaction to experiences with racism (Kibria, 2002). Korean-identified students at Academic High believed that if Koreans achieved model minority success they could overcome racism and gain greater acceptance in mainstream society. For these students, the coethnic networks were central to preserving the model minority image of Korean Americans. The peer networks worked to downplay and hide behaviors and experiences (e.g., low academic achievement) among Koreans that they feared might threaten the image of Korean Americans as model minorities. Finally, research has identified the central role of Korean protestant churches in the maintenance of a distinct Korean identity in the United States (Min, 1998; Park, 2004). As noted in Chapter 2, many of the Korean-identified students at AHS knew one another from the local Korean American community and some attended the same Korean church.

Korean-identified students overwhelmingly expressed pro-school attitudes, a finding consistent with the larger literature on Korean immigrants that points to the value that Korean immigrant parents place on education

(Kibria, 2002; Lew, 2006; Min, 1998). While academic achievement varied among Korean-identified students, none questioned the idea that education would help them achieve the American dream. That is, they held folk theories of success that linked education to social mobility (Ogbu, 1987, 1991, 1994).

As discussed in Chapter 3, the Korean-identified students' ethnic solidarity was evidenced in peer networks in which they shared information about school and helped one another with homework. More recent research has highlighted the fact that the social capital conferred by these peer networks is crucial to the school success of Korean immigrant youth (Lew, 2006; Park, 2007). For example, Lew (2006) discovered that high-achieving, middle-class Korean American students relied on one another for help and support with academics.

Like the archetypal immigrant described by Ogbu (1987, 1990, 1991, 1994), the Korean-identified students were generally optimistic about their lives in the United States. The Korean-identified students at AHS were the children of post-1965 immigrants, including many with parents who were middle-class professionals in Korea and came to the United States in search of greater economic opportunities and in search of educational opportunities for their children. According to Park (1997) the economic, political, and cultural influence of the United States in Korea has fostered an "American fever" among many Korean immigrants. Korean-identified students assume that through education they would achieve social mobility, which in turn would elevate their social and political status in the United States. Although hopeful about their prospects for success in the United States, Korean-identified students seemed to understand that Koreans would not be able to usurp the position of whites, and thus they chose to adapt the strategy of accommodation without assimilation in relation to the dominant culture (Gibson, 1988). They were aware of racism, but believed it could be overcome through hard work and accommodations to the dominant culture. Thus, their decision to acculturate to white middle-class norms was strategic.

Significantly, the identity formation of Korean-identified students suggests that social class is salient to ethnic and racial identity. Indeed, ethnic solidarity among Korean students at AHS was supported by the social class homogeneity of the students. Recent research on the Korean American community highlights the growing class bifurcation within the Korean immigrant population (Lew, 2006; Park, 2007). Lew, for example, found that the working-class Korean immigrants were not privy to the social capital enjoyed by their middle-class coethnics. Korean-identified students at AHS understood that social class was a significant variable in American society, and they sought to use their merchant status to distance themselves from working-class and poor Southeast Asians. The Korean-identified students marked their middle-class status by wearing clothes associated with upper-middle-class white students. Here, it is crucial to take note of the fact that they were intentionally adopting white youth styles, and not styles associated with urban youth of color (Perry, 2002). My point here is not to suggest that the Korean-identified students held prejudicial attitudes toward people of color, but to highlight the fact that they recognized that whites sit at the top of the racial hierarchy. Anthropologist Keyoung Park (1996) argues that Korean immigrant attitudes regarding race, particularly their respect for whites, have been influenced by Western economic, political, and military power and the "pervasive American cultural presence in South Korea, especially since the Korean War" (p. 494).

In other words, the Korean-identified students' rejection of pan-ethnicity was motivated by a fear that association with Southeast Asians might hurt their status. They did not want to be associated with Southeast Asians because they perceived them to be "drain[s] on the economy" and they likely understood that many whites were critical of people on public assistance. In other words, the Korean-identified students' upwardly mobile aspirations shaped their responses to the low-income Southeast Asian students. In short, Korean-identified students believed that their higher social-class status could attenuate the impact of racism. Indeed, economic self-sufficiency is a central characteristic of the model minority.

Despite the patterns that I observed among Korean American students, it is important to note that not all Korean American students at AHS were ethnic separatists. In fact, one of the central members of the Asian American–identified group was a Korean American student named Young (Chapter 5). As with other Asian American–identified students, Young embraced a pan-ethnic identity for political reasons. Like other students who adopted a pan-ethnic identity, Young remained connected to her specific ethnic identity as well. Young's case reminds us that all identity is fluid and responsive to social conditions. In general, the Korean-identified students' identity suggests that immigrant student identity is influenced by a group's beliefs about culture and identity, its historical experiences with outsiders, and its present social circumstances and interpretations of its position. Finally, recent research on Korean Americans calls attention to the significance of social class in ethnic networks and student achievement.

Asian-Identified Students

The students categorized as Asian-identified represented the largest group of Asian American students at Academic High. This group was diverse in terms of ethnicity and country of origin. In general, these students used both the pan-ethnic label of Asian and ethnic specific terms to describe themselves. As discussed in Chapter 2, a pan-ethnic identification provided these students with a social network from which they gained social, emotional, and practical support. These students did not see their Asian identities as overtly political, and did not engage in pan-Asian political activities. Rather, they spoke of their Asianness in terms of sharing similar struggles at the school and in the United States, and about sharing similar cultures. Asian-identified students believed that the Asian Students' Association should focus on cultural and educational events.

With respect to common "Asian" experiences, Asian-identified students asserted that Asian parents were stricter than non-Asian parents. Here, there was often joking about the high expectations Asian parents had regarding academic achievement, and about the strict rules Asian parents had for behavior. Asian-identified students also spoke about the challenges that Asian immigrants experienced in becoming fluent in English. Specifically, many Asian-identified students remarked that they were self-conscious about their Asian accents, and feared non-Asians would either not understand them and/or make fun of their accents if they spoke in class. Even very high-achieving Asian-identified students like Thai Le saw Asian-accented English as a barrier to future achievements. As noted in Chapter 5, Asian-identified students internalized the racist standards that marked Asian accents as inferior. Despite their concerns regarding their Asian accents, Asian-identified students usually spoke to one another in English because they came from diverse language backgrounds and English was their common language.

Common experiences with racism supported a pan-ethnic identity among Asian-identified students. In fact, all Asian-identified students reported being the victims of racial slurs, and some had been physically threatened; yet most were reluctant to challenge racism directly. For Asian-identified students the pan-ethnic identification provided a sense of safety that comes from being in a big group. Although Asian-identified students did not engage in political activism, their response to racism revealed a politics of accommodation that reflected their understanding that Asians are subordinate to whites. Like the Korean-identified students most Asian-identified students believed that Asians would gain greater acceptance and status by striving to be model minorities. For example, Thai Le believed that the status of Asians would rise if Asians "live[d] up to standards." It is important to point out that the strategy of embodying the model minority image is not unique to Asian- and Korean-identified students at AHS. In fact, there is ample evidence that various Asian groups have embraced the model minority image as a tactic for dealing with racism (Du, 2008; Wang, 2008).

The Asian-identified students' support of the model minority stereotype was one of the major differences between Asian-identified and Asian American–identified students. Students like Thai not only promoted the model minority image of Asians, but also suggested that the Asian American–identified students' criticisms of the model minority stereotype were wrong-headed and dangerous. Thai and other Asian-identified students criticized the Asian American–identified students for being too loud. They feared that the outspoken behavior of the Asian American–identified students would hurt the status of all Asian Americans. Here, the Asian-identified students' acceptance of the belief that "good Asians are quiet" represented a consent to hegemony.

The Asian-identified students' image of themselves as model minorities also informed their attitudes toward other groups of people of color. As noted in Chapter 5, high achieving Asian-identified students asserted that affirmative action policies unfairly favored African Americans and discriminated against Asians. The attitudes of these students highlight the fact that the position of Asian Americans as a model minority is contingent upon the stereotype of African Americans as the failing minority. Given the generally neoconservative positions advanced by these students, it is certainly reasonable to imagine that as college students some of these students may have been involved in the pan-Asian activism against affirmative action that emerged in the 1990s.

The Asian-identified students expressed pro-school attitudes and behaviors that were central to their model minority self-presentations. These students were respectful toward teachers and were generally described in positive terms by their teachers. Although Asian-identified students experienced varied levels of academic achievement they all asserted the importance of getting an education. In fact, Asian-identified students viewed education as being the best protection against racism, an idea they had learned from their parents. Similarly, in her research on Chinese immigrant college students, Louie (2004) found that immigrant parents emphasize the centrality of education in attenuating the impact of racial discrimination on their children. In the process of trying to live up to the model minority stereotype, Asian-identified students silenced behaviors and experiences that failed to measure up to the model minority standards. Like the Korean-identified students, Asian-identified students believed in the possibility of achieving the American dream through hard work and talent. Although this identity category included refugees who did not come to the United States voluntarily, all Asian-identified students held folk theories of success associated with immigrants regarding the role of education in social mobility (Ogbu, 1987, 1990, 1991).

Significantly, Asian-identified students noted that their parents did not express pan-ethnic identities and did not see Asians as having shared concerns. There is considerable evidence that when Asian immigrants first arrive in the United States they have a strong preference for ethnic-only identities like the ones expressed by Korean-identified students and Taiwanese American students. Asian immigrants have historically established ethnic-specific social and political organizations upon arrival in the United States. Post–1965 Chinese immigrants, for example, have established ethnic organizations in Chinatowns and new "ethnoburbs" that support adaptation to the United States and the maintenance of ethnic ties (Zhou & Kim, 2006). Length of time in the United States, particularly repeated experiences with racial subordination and racialization as Asians, promotes the formation of pan-ethnic identity among Asians (Okamoto, 2003). Common experiences at AHS and in their communities led Asian-identified students to form pan-ethnic identities.

Although Asian-identified students embraced pan-ethnic identities when around non-Asians, they often displayed their specific ethnic identities among themselves. Taiwanese American students, in particular, mentioned that they empathized with the Korean-identified students' desire to be seen as separate from other Asian Americans. Like the Korean-identified students, the few Taiwanese American students at Academic High were from merchant/middle-class backgrounds and inclined to believe that their social-class status meant that they were superior to working-class Asian Americans. While the Korean-identified students had a sizeable cohort of coethnics, there were only a few Taiwanese American students at AHS, and the small number of coethnics appeared to limit their ability to assert a separate Taiwanese identity. Given the situation at AHS, the Taiwanese students chose to identify as Taiwanese and as Asian. Like the other Asian-identified students, Taiwanese American students hoped that by working together with other Asian ethnic groups they could work to educate nonwhites about Asians. The Taiwanese American students' dilemma suggests that the population size of individual ethnic groups may influence the identity process.

In the nearly 20 years since my fieldwork at Academic High I have encountered many Asian American students who have reminded me of the Asian-identified students at Academic High. Although most of these students do not express pan-ethnic identities, they share similar aspirations, behaviors, and attitudes with the Asian-identified students. In my fieldwork in the Midwest and in large urban school districts in the Northeast I have met Asian American students who, like the Asian-identified students, are generally quiet, hardworking, and politically and socially conservative. For example, in my ethnographic research on Hmong American youth at a high school in Wisconsin, I found that students who were identified as "traditional" paid attention to their studies, obeyed and respected their parents, and followed school rules (Lee, 2005). Although they experienced varied levels of academic achievement, most maintained an unquestioned belief that education was the best route to social mobility. In short, like the Asian-identified students at Academic High, the "traditional" Hmong students and other quiet Asian American students around the country appear to confirm much of the model minority image of Asian Americans. As the Asian-identified students' case demonstrates, however, behind this veneer are complexities that trouble the model minority stereotype.

New Wavers

Like the Asian-identified students, new wave students' pan-ethnicity was informed by their understanding that Asians from a range of ethnic groups share a common position relative to non-Asians. Although these students recognized some cultural and historical differences among Asians, they agreed that being "Asian" was different from being white, African American, Latino, or Native American. In particular, new wave students argued that Asians needed to stick together because they were less politically, economically, and socially powerful than whites, and less socially powerful than African Americans. Although they were more likely than their Asian-identified peers to express anger regarding racism and racial inequality, new wavers did not participate in organized pan-Asian politics. For new wavers, a pan-ethnic identity provided an important form of social support and practical protection from the real potential of racially charged altercations. Like Asian-identified students, the new wavers displayed pan-ethnic identities among non-Asians, and often referred to their specific ethnic identities among themselves.

In striking contrast to the Asian- and Korean-identified students, the new wavers rejected the model minority image. New wave students feared that the model minority stereotype contributed to the image that Asians are nerds. Here, it was clear that new wavers believed that the nerd image hurt the social position of Asian students among non-Asian peers, and placed Asians at risk for being ridiculed, attacked, and abused. Influenced by their desire to reject the nerd image, new wavers resisted all behavior associated with the stereotype, including open investment in schooling. As noted in Chapter 2, new wave students made efforts to appear mature and worldly and they viewed following school rules to be a sign of immaturity. Most significantly, new wave boys believed that the model minority stereotype and the associated nerd image contributed to the stereotype of Asian men as being effeminate. Asian American scholars have highlighted the concerns regarding emasculation faced by Asian American men and boys, and the new wave boys appeared to be painfully aware that Asian boys were perceived by others to be small and weak (Eng, 2001; Kumashiro, 1999). Numerous scholars have pointed to the relationship between conceptualizations of gender and attitudes toward education, in particular the belief among some working-class and poor youth that education is femininizing and therefore threatens masculinity (Carter, 2005; Willis, 1977). Carter (2005), for example, found that the African American and Latino boys in her study were under a great deal of social pressure to be "hard" (i.e., tough), and that some boys had come to view aspects of schooling as "soft" (i.e., feminine). Although new wave boys did not explicitly state that they viewed education to be feminizing, they were intent on proving their masculinity by rejecting nerd-like behavior (i.e., studying and following rules) that might further challenge their masculinity. In other words, one reason the new wave boys rejected the model minority image was because they feared that it threatened their masculinity. I am not suggesting that the new wavers fully understood the racism behind the model minority stereotype, but I would argue that the new wavers held initial insights into how the stereotype influenced their experiences.

Like the other Asian American students at AHS, new wave students stated that their parents emphasized the importance of school in achieving success in the United States. Unlike the other Asian American students, however, new wavers did not accept the achievement ideology espoused by their parents. The new wavers' oppositional response to schooling challenges the assumption that newcomers to the United States remain optimistic about opportunities in the United States and believe in education as the best route to social mobility (Ogbu, 1987, 1991). It is important to remember that central to the cultural ecological theorists' explanation for immigrant students' achievement is their assumption that immigrant children hold the same values and attitudes toward education as their immigrant parents. For example, in writing about the influence that immigrant parents have over their children, Ogbu (1991) asserted:

> Parents and community members tend to insist that children follow school rules of behavior that enhance academic success. For their part, immigrant minority children seem to respond positively to their parents' advice and training and to parental and community pressure. (p. 22)

Despite their parents' entreaties regarding the importance of education, new wavers questioned the value of formal education in their lives. In particular, new wave students questioned whether anything learned in school could protect them on the streets. Negative experiences with the police and security officers at the mall led them to distrust authority figures and attacked their confidence in the fairness of mainstream institutions, including schools. New wavers suggested that their parents held idealistic ideas about education, and didn't understand the issues that teens faced in school or in the larger American society. Ultimately, the new wavers' distrust of educational institutions contributed to their academic difficulties.

Significantly, new wavers' ambivalence toward school developed during their time at Academic High. They reported that prior to high school they had liked school and had been good students, but negative experiences in the hypercompetitive culture of AHS had led them to dislike and distrust school. Cultural ecological theorists and scholars who have advanced ideas regarding segmented assimilation have downplayed the role of schools in student responses to school (Ogbu, 1991; Zhou & Bankston, 1998). Ogbu stated, "Although immigrant minorities may be attending segregated and/or inferior schools, their overall evaluation of their educational opportunity is not disillusioned" (p. 21). However, my research at Academic High suggests that the school played a central role in the formation of the new wavers' oppositional identity. In other words, school cultures, policies, and practices influence the way in which students respond to school. Recent research supports my argument that oppositional identities are formed in response to the actions of schools (Tyson, 2002; Valenzuela, 1999). Tyson (2002), for example, found that black children enter school with pro-school attitudes, but develop negative attitudes over time in response to experiences in school.

There is significant evidence that the oppositional identity expressed by the new wavers is growing among second-generation Asian American youth from working-class and poor backgrounds (Lee, 2005; McGinnis, 2007; Reyes, 2007; Zhou & Bankston, 1998). In their research on Vietnamese students, Zhou and Bankston (1998) found that while most Vietnamese students were successful, a growing number of second-generation Vietnamese youth were engaging in delinquent behavior. According to Zhou and Bankston (1998) these delinquent youth have lost their culture and have assimilated into the urban youth culture. While Zhou and Bankston's (1998) work presaged an important trend among low-income Asian American immigrant youth, they did not address the issue of why the youth are attracted to an oppositional urban youth culture.

In my research on Hmong American youth I found that students' experiences with poverty, racism, and unresponsive schools all contributed to oppositional attitudes (Lee, 2001, 2003, 2004). Interestingly, many second-generation Hmong American students adopted hip-hop styles of dress and speech, which mainstream educators and the students themselves associated with African American urban youth. Indeed, these students adopted a hip-hop aesthetic because they viewed hip-hop as expressing a critique of racial and class inequality. Furthermore, these students identified more with the status of African American students than with middle-class white students at the school (Lee, 2005). Similarly, in her ethnographic study of an after-school program for Southeast Asian youth in Philadelphia, Reyes (2007) discovered that for Southeast Asian adolescents "African American identity was often associated with their present and future" (p. 62). The Southeast Asian youth in her study identified with African American experiences, and were drawn to and participated in the hip-hop culture associated with African American urban youth.

Finally, recent research suggests that some low-income Asian American boys may be adopting hop-hop styles in order to gain a more masculine or hypermasculine image (Lee, 2005; Lei, 2003). Lei (2003) discovered that Southeast Asian boys' decision to enact a more masculine identity through hip-hop styles had unintended consequences, including being cast as deviant by teachers.

> By choosing to adopt markers associated with black masculinity, which has been stereotyped as hypermasculine and a threat to white male prerogative (Ferguson, 2000), the Southeast Asian American male students gained a tougher image. However, this tougher image also materialized them as deviant academic and social beings. (p. 177)

Thus, the experiences of the new wave boys at Academic High and the experiences of Asian American boys in more recent studies (Lee, 2005; Lei, 2003) highlight the importance of gender in Asian American student identities.

While it might have been tempting to see new wave students as exceptions to the norm, recent research suggests otherwise. The fact that oppositional behaviors are increasingly being expressed by working-class Asian American youth underscores the fact that students' lived experiences in school and in communities shape identities.

Asian American–Identified Students

Although pan-ethnicity among Asian- and new wave–identified students was largely reactive and protective, for Asian American–identified students pan-ethnicity was not simply reactive, but also proactive. These students reclaimed the Asian American pan-ethnic label as a source of pride, solidarity, and strength. The Korean, Chinese, and Vietnamese students who identified as Asian American were concerned with various forms of inequality, and argued that issues of race and class were connected. Asian American–identified students were outspoken in their critique of the model minority stereotype. While the new wavers' complaints regarding the stereotype were largely intuitive, the Asian American students' critique was very focused. They rejected the model minority stereotype as racist propaganda, charging that it was inaccurate and harmful to interracial relationships between Asian Americans and other racial minorities. They believed that, as racial minorities, they shared things in common with all people of color, and asserted that coalition building across racial groups would strengthen the fight for social justice. As noted in Chapter 5, Asian American–identified students worked with students in the Black Student Union to organize the workshop on black-Asian relations.

Asian American–identified girls argued that gender and race were equally significant in their lives, and they suggested that many Asian-identified boys held "traditional" attitudes regarding gender. Stephen Chau, a gay student who first identified as Asian and later as Asian American, shifted identities because of experiences with homophobia within the Asian-identified community. Within the Asian American–identified community Stephen found greater acceptance, and was able to come to peace with the various parts of his identity.

The identity expressed by Asian American–identified students is reminiscent of the identity expressed by those involved in the Asian American movement of the 1960s. In his analysis of the Asian American movement of the 1960s, Wei (2004) explains that pan-Asian activists were "inspired both by their African American and Latino peers and by Third World liberation movements and the Cultural Revolution in China" (p. 300). The goals of the early Asian American movement were to advocate for the rights of Asian Americans. One of the central achievements of the 1960s Asian American movement was the development of Asian American Studies as an academic field. Some of the most outspoken Asian American–identified students at AHS were active participants in an Asian American community group staffed by politically progressive Asian American adults, including some who expressed the political discourse of the 1960s Asian American movement. The community group engaged in a range of political activities (e.g., educational advocacy for low-income Asian American immigrant and refugee students, housing rights for low-income families, immigrant rights), and encouraged youth to become politically active in their communities.

In recent years, the pan-Asian movement has continued to evolve as the Asian American population has become more diverse with the influx of newer immigrants and refugees (Wei, 2004). While there are still some Asian American activists who express the politics associated with the

1960s, many of today's Asian American activists are more politically conservative. As noted in the section on Asian-identified students, some of the more outspoken Asian-identified students were beginning to voice the perspective of the more politically conservative Asian American activists. The split in the Asian American community regarding affirmative action best represents the political divide in the current pan-Asian movement (Robles, 2006; Wei, 2004).

Arguably the most interesting thing about the Asian American–identified students is that their identity represents a direct challenge to Ogbu's suggestion that the recognition of racism threatens students' commitment to education. Like the immigrant minorities described by Ogbu (1987, 1991), Gibson (1988, 1991), and Suárez-Orozco (1991), the Asian American–identified students were academically successful. In fact, they were all college-bound and were among the highest-achieving students at the school. Unlike the typical immigrant minority, however, they articulated a keen understanding of the racial dynamics at Academic High and in the United States. Ogbu (1991) did not deal with students who recognize racism and continue to strive to do well in school. In fact, he assumed that awareness of racism and distrust of schools puts students at risk for oppositional attitudes and underachievement. For example, Ogbu (1991) asserted, "The deep distrust that involuntary minorities have for members of the dominant group and the schools they control adds to the minorities' difficulties in school" (p. 28).

Asian American–identified students believed that racism was a reality that all people of color faced, and they recognized that even highly educated Asian Americans experienced racism. Furthermore, they believed that schools were implicated in the reproduction of inequality. Despite their skepticism regarding the ability of schools to provide full equality, Asian American–identified students planned to use their education to fight and resist both personal and institutional racism. The Asian American–identified students learned that education could be harnessed in the fight against inequality by observing the actions of their adult role models in the Asian American community group. Many of these adults held advanced degrees and used the knowledge they gained from formal education to fight racial and class inequality faced by Asian Americans.

Recent research has focused attention on the relationship between attitudes toward education and acknowledgment of racial and class barriers. In her research on low-income Latino and African American high school students, Carter (2005) found that the majority of cultural mainstreamers (i.e., students who comply with school norms), cultural straddlers (i.e., students who negotiate multiple cultures), and noncompliant students (i.e., those who do not comply with school norms) believed that job discrimination exists, a fact that suggests that there is not a simple one-to-one relationship between perceptions of racism and attitudes toward education. O'Connor (1997), for example, identified a group of high-achieving African American students who expressed pro-school attitudes despite the fact that they recognized the racial and class constraints they faced. Like the Asian American–identified students, these "resilient" youth had adult role models who demonstrated how they could negotiate racial and class barriers.

"Other" Asians: South Asian American Students at Academic High

In reviewing my data nearly 20 years later I realized that there was one group of Asian American students whom I neglected to write about in the 1996 edition of this book—South Asians. During my research at Academic High there were a few South Asian students—Indian and Pakistani—in attendance. Early in my research I interviewed two South Asian students, but I didn't end up pursuing research with the South Asian students because they didn't appear to identify with the Asian category, and East Asian and Southeast Asian students did not perceive South Asians to be Asian. The Asian American–identified students were the only ones to recognize South Asians as part of the Asian American category, but they did not socialize with any South Asian students.

The two South Asian students I did interview used ethnic-specific terms to describe themselves, and suggested that they did not relate to the Asian American category. I didn't think to ask them whether they identified with the label "South Asian," a contested term among those it is meant to include (Bahri & Vasudeva, 1996; Maira, 2001; Rudrappa, 2004). Interestingly, these two students were aware of the model minority stereotype and explained that South Asians were also seen as model minorities. More recent research confirms that South Asian students must contend with the model minority stereotype (Asher, 2002). Both of the students I interviewed were born in the United States to middle-class immigrant parents, and socialized primarily with middle-class white students. When asked about their friendship patterns they explained that they were "Americanized," which I understood to mean that they were comfortable in white middle-class society.

The relationship between South Asians and other Asian Americans has been an issue of scholarly debate within Asian American studies. Some researchers have argued that South Asians have been excluded from the Asian American movement, and others have suggested that being subsumed by the Asian American identity may, in fact, be dangerous for South Asians (Bahri, 1998; Kibria, 2000). Kibria (2000) observes that

South Asians are ambiguous nonwhites who do not fit neatly into the racial categories recognized by the dominant racial discourse. Research on South Asian youth reveals that South Asians are often mistaken for other groups, including Latinos and mixed-raced blacks (Sandhu, 2004). Kibria (2000) argues that "perceived racial difference between South Asians and other Asian Americans" may play a significant role in the social distance between South Asians and other Asian Americans (p. 252). Unfortunately, I did not ask East Asians or Southeast Asians whether skin color played any role in their exclusion of South Asians from the Asian category. According to Academic High's current Web site there is currently an active "Indian Pakistani Cultural Club" at the school. Given the political tensions between India and Pakistan, the name of the club is particularly interesting, and an ethnographer conducting research on Asian American identities at Academic High today would be wise to include a discussion of this group and South Asian students in general. I must admit that I wish I had included the South Asian students in my research back in 1989.

FINAL THOUGHTS
ON IDENTITY AND RESPONSES TO EDUCATION

My fieldwork at Academic High School confirmed my initial assumption that the identity process is influenced by interracial contact. As I argued throughout this book, the model minority stereotype greatly influenced race relations between Asians and non-Asians. Identity formation among Asian American students was also influenced by how they interpreted their status relative to non-Asian and Asian groups, by their perceptions of future opportunities, by issues of social class, and by a myriad of other factors. Importantly, identity formation was also influenced by their intra-Asian relationships. All these factors played a role in whether students embraced pan-ethnic/racial identity as Asian or Asian American.

The fact that Asian American students at Academic High formed their ethnic and racial identities in response to their perceived conditions and social locations supports the idea that ethnic identity is motivated by self-interest and that ethnic groups are at least in part interest groups. Culture, however, was not a completely unimportant aspect of ethnic identity. Asian American students who identified as Korean, Asian, and new wave made references to the significance of cultural distinctions in marking them as different from non-Asians. Asian- and new wave–identified students watched me for signs of cultural competence (e.g., speaking Chinese, eating Chinese food, wearing jade) in order to determine my "Asianness." Despite references to culture, however, cultural differences and similarities were less important to ethnic identity than issues of power.

The varied academic achievement among Asian American students at Academic High challenges simplistic characterizations of Asian Americans as model minorities. The students' varied responses to school revealed complexities that are masked by the cultural ecological theory. While my study included immigrants (i.e., voluntary minorities) and refugees (i.e., semivoluntary), the variation in achievement and attitudes toward school could not be explained by these differences in categories. That is, there were high- and low-achieving immigrant students and high- and low-achieving refugee students. Cultural ecological theorists assumed that immigrant parents and their children share similar ideas regarding life in the United States, thereby underestimating the significance of generational differences. New wave students and Asian American–identified students' interpretations of racism and their understandings of education differed from that of their families. Finally, my data demonstrated that the new wave students' oppositional attitudes and behaviors were informed by their experiences at Academic High. Thus, this research sits alongside more recent research that demonstrates the profound ways that school policies, practices, and cultures shape immigrant students' experiences and responses to school, and their understandings of where they fit in the broader society (Conchas, 2001; Lee, 2005; Lopez, 2003; Sarroub, 2005; Suárez-Orozco & Suárez-Orozco, 2001; Valenzuela, 1999).

ISSUES OF RACE

As in the larger society, most non-Asians at Academic High School accepted the accuracy of the model minority stereotype, and assumed that Asian Americans inside and outside of AHS were academically and economically successful. Although white and African American students at AHS identified Asian Americans as high achievers, their attitudes toward Asian Americans and Asian American success depended on their relative position in the school, in their communities, and in the dominant society. In other words, a racial group's perceptions of their own social, economic, and political positions informed their attitudes toward Asians/Asian Americans and Asian American success.

At Academic High, white students were widely recognized among African American, Asian American, and white students as having the most social status at the school. White students were well represented in the academic elite, and in the high-status extracurricular activities. And finally, white students made up 45% of the student population, making them the single largest racial group at the school. Thus, white students were secure in their position at the top of the racial hierarchy. As such, most whites were not threatened by Asian American success, and most held relatively positive attitudes toward Asian Americans. Indeed, the majority of white students at Academic High talked about Asian American success in positive terms. According to some white students and teachers, Asian American students were model minorities who proved that equal opportunity existed for students of all races.

Asian American writers, scholars, and activists have repeatedly warned us that the model minority stereotype is an expression of racist love, and therefore is dependent on the dominant group's perception of their own position relative to Asian Americans. Cho (1993) writes, "Because the embrace or love is not genuine, one cannot reasonably expect the architects truly to care about the health or well-being of the model minority" (p. 203). In other words, when whites are secure in their status, Asian American success is seen as positive, but when whites feel threatened Asian American success is unwanted competition. Several studies suggest that when whites feel that their status is threatened, they begin to view Asian American success and achievement as negative (Fong, 1994; Newman, 1993; Takagi, 1992). Under these circumstances, Asian Americans are no longer viewed as "model minorities" but are instead viewed as potential dominators. Katherine Newman's (1993) study of downward mobility among middle-class whites suggests that when whites feel that their status is threatened, they turn their anger on Asians. Thus, attitudes of whites toward Asians are directly influenced by perceptions of their own status. Fong's (1994) study of Monterey Park, California, also suggests that whites' attitudes toward Asian success can turn from positive to negative. Fong reports that the large immigrant Chinese population "changed the demographic, economic, social, cultural, and political landscape" of Monterey Park, and he asserts that one result of these changes has been an increase in anti-Asian sentiment.

More recently there have been reports of white flight in Silicon Valley in response to the growth in middle- and upper-middle-class Asian American population in local public schools (Hwang, 2005). Reporting on the trend in one community, one journalist observed, "Some white Cupertino parents are instead sending their children to private schools or moving them to other, whiter public schools. More commonly, young white families in Silicon Valley say they are avoiding Cupertino altogether" (Hwang, 2005, p. 1). According to this article, white parents in Silicon Valley have expressed concern that Asian American students are too competitive and that their own children end up being stereotyped as underachievers in contrast to the hyperachievement-oriented Asian

American students. In short, the white parents fear that their children can't compete against the Asian American students. Thus, within the white imagination, Asian Americans have been transformed from model minorities into Mongol hordes.

At Academic High, the white, working-class students from the south side of the city (i.e., the East Lawners) were outsiders within the white student group. East Lawners kept largely to themselves, and were criticized by high-achieving white students for being racist. As noted in Chapter 5, even the principal suggested that the East Lawners were racially intolerant. It is important to remember that both East Lawners and Asian American students were outsiders at the school, and that both groups were competing to gain respect within the school. Like others who felt threatened, East Lawners equated Asian success with Asian dominance. Their fear of Asian dominance translated into hostility toward all Asians. Other signs of anti-Asian sentiment among white students at Academic High were beginning to be expressed by a few high-achieving students, most of whom were middle class. These students asserted that Asians were "not normal" because all they did was study. Jennifer Smith, a high-achieving white student, pointed out that she and her friends, unlike the Asian American students, were good students but also "normal" people who did other things besides study. The image of Asian American students as "unfair competitors" is common among white college students who attend colleges where Asians represent a significant portion of the student population. Some of these white students report that they avoid classes where there are too many Asians because Asians ruin the curve (Takagi, 1992). The attitudes expressed by these high-achieving, middle-class white students demonstrate that working-class whites are not inherently more racist than middle-class whites, as some individuals at AHS suggested. Rather, this data suggests that racism is likely to be expressed by whites across class backgrounds when Asian competition becomes a threat.

In general, the relationships between Asian American students and African American students were tense. Most Asian American students viewed African Americans with suspicion. Korean-, new wave-, and Asian-identified students accepted the stereotype that many African Americans are lazy welfare recipients. High-achieving, Asian-identified students resented African Americans because they believed that African Americans received unfair advantages through affirmative action programs. The Korean-identified, new wave-identified, and Asian-identified students' negative attitudes toward African Americans were a product of their relative structural positions in society. For the most part, the Korean-identified and Asian-identified students were relative newcomers to this country who believed that equal opportunity existed for all races. They justified the racism experienced by African Americans by blaming the victims. Their rationalization of the injustices experienced by African Americans preserved their belief in the fairness of the system. Furthermore, Korean-identified, new wave–identified, and Asian-identified students recognized that African Americans are beneath whites in the racial hierarchy, and they feared that association with African Americans might hurt their own status. Recent research confirms that immigrants may distance themselves from African Americans in their efforts to achieve upward mobility in mainstream society (Islam, 2000; Waters, 1999).

For their part, most African American students perceived Asian American "success as anything but positive. African American students accused Asian Americans of economic exploitation. According to the majority of African American students, all Asians were guilty of getting rich by buying up stores in African American neighborhoods. Thus, while the dominant group saw Asian entrepreneurship as evidence that Asian Americans are model minorities, African American students viewed Asian entrepreneurship as evidence of Asian domination. The economic tensions between African Americans and Asian Americans have been expressed in popular culture. Shortly after my fieldwork at Academic High, for example, rapper Ice Cube issued a warning to Korean merchants in African American neighborhoods. The tension between African Americans and Asian Americans has been the subject of much academic discourse (Kim, 2000).

At least one scholar, however, has argued that both the media and the social science research has overexaggerated the conflict between African Americans and Asian Americans (Lie, 2004). In challenging the conflict thesis that has dominated the literature on Korean American–African American relations, Lie (2004) argues that the two groups have not been in direct competition for employment, housing, or political power. Although Lie acknowledges the existence of individual prejudice on both sides, he points out that reports of conflict have focused exclusively on relations between Korean merchants and black customers and that very little evidence exists for general conflict between the groups. Recent research on Asian American youth, which highlights the affinity that many low-income Asian American youth are expressing toward African American youth culture, certainly suggests that relations between African Americans and Asian Americans are filled with complexities and contradictions (Lee, 2005; Reyes, 2007).

At Academic High, however, African American students and Asian American students were perceived to be competitors, a perception rooted in the school's history. As noted in Chapter 4, during the late 1980s the African American student population at Academic High dropped and the Asian American student population grew. Given the special status of Academic High within the city, the shift in the racial makeup of the school was symbolically important. The growth in the Asian American population did reflect the significant growth in the Asian American population in the entire school district. Some observers, however, asserted that the drop in the African American population and the growth in the Asian American population reflected the admissions policies put in place by the principal. Inside the halls of Academic High policies regarding tracking and ranking further fueled competition between the groups. African Americans were locked out of the academic elite, and they interpreted Asian American students' success as confirmation of their fears that Asians are taking over everything. Their perceptions of Asian Americans as highly successful (i.e., model minorities and fierce competitors) were confirmed by the number of Asians in the top tracks, the number of Asians ranked in the top ten of each graduating class, and teachers' rhetoric about Asian students being smart. In this way, the stereotype of Asian Americans as high achievers and the stereotype that Asians are fierce competitors who are taking over became blurred.

Although issues outside of the school informed the tension between African American and Asian American students at Academic High, it is clear that the school added to the racial tensions through its culture of competition. For example, my data suggests that Academic High's policy of ranking students each year and its policy of posting the names of the top ten students in each grade was unnecessary and negatively influenced race relations. One high-achieving, Asian American–identified student who was sensitive to the interracial tension at Academic criticized the school's policy of posting the rankings: "They [non-Asians] see all the Asians up there—it's really striking. It causes resentment. People don't realize that not all Asians do that well." In the class of 1990, the top 10 students included six Asian American students. The posting of these rankings added credibility to the model minority stereotype. Like Mrs. Lewis, the African American teacher discussed in Chapter 4, I would argue that much of the tracking at Academic High is redundant and unnecessary. Tracking at Academic High led to the resegregation of students and negatively affected interracial relations. Thus, while I do not believe that the school was directly responsible for the interracial tension between students, I do believe that the school contributed to the interracial tensions through its policies. Furthermore, my data suggests that the school should have made changes to improve relations between African American and Asian American students.

Finally, recent reports of conflict between Asian and non-Asian students in schools across the country suggest that scholars should not ignore the way that race influences social interaction. In one widely publicized case of conflict between blacks and Asians at Lafayette High School in Bensonhurst, New York, Chinese and Pakistani immigrant youth were repeatedly the targets of anti-Asian violence (AALDEF, 2005). Given that Asian Americans are regularly compared to other groups, we need to pay attention to how schools influence relationships between Asian American and non-Asian students. What role do racial stereotypes, including the model minority stereotype, play in relationships between Asian American and non-Asian youth? How do policies such as tracking influence attitudes toward Asian American students?

FINAL REFLECTIONS
ON THE MODEL MINORITY STEREOTYPE

June 26, 1989—It is late in the year and the class of 1989 has just graduated. The juniors are excited about becoming seniors, and freshman seem simply elated that they will no longer be freshman come the fall. I'm tired from months in the field, but a little sorry that my daily visits to Academic High will soon come to an end. I decide to make a final visit to the computer room where many of the high-achieving, Asian-identified male students gather on a regular basis. As I sit talking to Mr. Engen, the teacher in charge of the computer room, the subject of Asian American student achievement surfaces. Mr. Engen is bubbling over with praise for his Asian American students. After listening for some minutes, I decide to question his understanding of Asian Americans as model minorities. Mr. Engen understands that I am critical of the stereotype, but before I can complete my thought, he stops me and says, "Please don't ruin my stereotype. It is such a nice one." Thus, once again, I learn one of the secrets to the endurance of the model minority stereotype.

I have been writing about the dangers of the model minority stereotype for nearly 20 years, and in that time I have encountered a great deal of resistance from both non-Asians and Asians who insist that the stereotype is both accurate and positive. What could be wrong with being characterized as industrious, smart, and successful? Indeed, some Asian Americans may enjoy certain privileges associated with being seen as model minorities, but the Academic High case demonstrates the problematic nature of the stereotype. As in the larger society, the model minority stereotype was used at Academic High to silence claims of racial inequality. The stereotype set standards for how Asian American students and all other students of color should behave, and it hid the problems faced by some Asian American students. And finally, the stereotype influenced the way Asian American students viewed themselves, and when that happens, they may, as one student reminds us, "just lose your identity . . . lose being yourself." Thus, in response to the model minority stereotype, we must ask the following questions: Who benefits from the stereotype? What ideologies are supported? Who is hurt and/or hidden by the stereotype?

References

Ancheta, A. (2003). *Race, rights, and the Asian American experience*. New Brunswick, NJ: Rutgers University Press.

Apple, M. W. (1993). Constructing the "other": Rightist reconstruction of common sense. In C. McCarthy & W. Crichlow (Eds.), *Race, identity, and representation in education* (pp. 24–39). New York: Routledge.

Apple, M. W. (2001). *Educating the "right way."* New York: Routledge.

Apple, M. W. (2004). Creating difference: Neo-liberalism, neo-conservatism and the politics of educational reform. *Educational Policy, 18,* 12–44.

Asher, N. (2002). Class acts: Indian American high school students negotiate professional and ethnic identities. *Urban Education, 37*(2), 267–295.

Asian American Legal Defense and Education Fund (AALDEF). (2005). *Lafayette High gets failing grade.* Retrieved July 25, 2008, from http://www.aaldef.org/articles/2005-01-01_334_AALDEFWinter20.pdf

Asian American Legal Defense and Education Fund (AALDEF). (2008). *Left in the margins: Asian American students and the No Child Left Behind Act.* New York: Author.

Au, K. H., & Jordan, C. (1981). Teaching reading to Hawaiian children: Finding a culturally appropriate solution. In H. T. Trueba, G. P. Guthrie, & K. H. Au (Eds.), *Culture in the bilingual classroom: Studies in classroom ethnography* (pp. 139–152). Rowley, MA: Newberry House.

Bahri, D. (1998). With kaleidoscope eyes: The potential (dangers) of identitarian coalitions. In L. Shankar (Ed.), *A part yet apart: South Asians in Asian America.* Philadelphia: Temple University Press.

Bahri, D., & Vasudeva, M. (1996). Introduction. In D. Bahri & M. Vasudeva (Eds.), *Between the lines: South Asians and postcoloniality* (pp. 1–6). Philadelphia: Temple University Press.

Bascara, V. (2006). *Model minority imperialism.* Minneapolis: University of Minnesota Press.

Brand, D. (1987, August 31). The new whiz kids. *Time, 130*(9), 42–51.

Brimelow, P. (1995). *Alien nation: Common sense about America's immigration disaster.* New York: Random House.

Burch, P. (2009). *Hidden markets: The new education privatization.* New York: Routledge.

Caplan, N., Choy, M. H., & Whitmore, J. K. (1991). *Children of the boat people. A study of educational success.* Ann Arbor: University of Michigan Press.

CARE (National Commission on Asian American and Pacific Islander Research in Education) & College Board. (2008). *Asian Americans and Pacific Islanders: Facts, not fiction: Setting the record straight.* Retrieved October 18, 2008, from http://www.nyu.edu/projects/care/CARE_Report-Revised.pdf

Carter, P. (2005). *Keepin' it real: School success beyond black and white.* New York: Oxford University Press.

Caudill, W., & De Vos, G. (1956). Achievement, culture and personality: The case of the Japanese Americans. *American Anthropologist, 58*(6), 1102–1127.

Centri, C. (1993, April). *Model minority stereotypes and the acceptance of inner city urban culture: The identity formation of Vietnamese high school students.* Paper presented at the annual meeting of the American Education Studies Association, Chicago.

Chang, J. (1993). Race, class, conflict and empowerment: On Ice Cube's "black Korea." *Amerasia Journal, 19*(2), 87–107.

Chang, R. (1993). Toward an Asian American legal scholarship: Critical race theory, post-structuralism, and narrative. *California Law Review, 81*(1241), 1243–1323.

Cheung, K. (1990). The woman warrior versus the Chinaman pacific: Must a Chinese American critic choose between feminism and heroism? In M. Hirsch & E. E. Keller (Eds.), *Conflicts in feminism* (pp. 234–251). New York: Routledge.

Cheung, K. (1993). *Articulate silences: Hisaye Yamamoto, Maxine Hong Kingston, Joy Kogawa.* Ithaca, NY: Cornell University Press.

Cho, S. K. (1993). Korean Americans vs. African Americans: Conflict and construction. In R. Gooding-Williams (Ed.), *Reading Rodney King/reading urban uprising* (pp. 196–211). New York: Routledge.

Chou, R., & Feagin, J. (2008). *The myth of the model minority: Asian Americans facing racism.* Boulder, CO: Paradigm Publishers.

Clark, K. B., & Clark, M. E. (1947). Racial identification and preference in Negro children. In T. M. Newcomb & E. L. Hartley (Eds.), *Readings in social psychology* (pp. 169–178). New York: Holt.

Committee of 100. (2001). *American attitudes toward Chinese Americans and Asian Americans: A Committee 100 survey.* New York: Author.

Conchas, G. (2001). Structuring failure and success: Understanding the variability in Latino school engagement. *Harvard Educational Review, 70*(3), 475–504.

Cornell, S. E. (1988). *The return of the native: American Indian political resurgence.* New York: Oxford University Press.

Dillabough, J., Kennelly, J., & Wang, E. (2008). Spatial containment in the inner city: Youth subcultures, class conflict, and geographies of exclusion. In L. Weis (Ed.), *The way class works: Readings on school, family, and the economy* (pp. 329–346). New York: Routledge.

Du, L. (2008). Community, ethnic identity, and social discourse: Case study of the impact of the model minority myth on a suburban Chinese American community. In G. Li & L. Wang (Eds.), *Model minority myth revisited: An interdisciplinary approach to demystifying Asian American educational experiences* (pp. 65–88). Charlotte, NC: Information Age Publishing.

Dyer, R. (1993). *The matter of images: Essays on representations.* New York: Routledge.

Eckert, E. (1989). *Jocks and burnouts: Social categories and identity in the high school.* New York: Teachers College Press.

Eng, D. (2001). *Racial castration: Managing masculinity in Asian America*. Durham, NC: Duke University Press.

Erickson, E. (1987). Transformation and school success: The politics and culture of educational achievement. *Anthropology & Education Quarterly, 18*(4), 335–356.

Erickson, E. D., & Mohatt, G. (1982). Cultural organization of participation structures in two classrooms of Indian students. In G. D. Spindler (Ed.), *Doing the ethnography of schooling: Educational anthropology in action* (pp. 132–175). New York: Holt, Rinehart & Winston.

Erickson, E., & Shultz, J. (1982). *The counselor as gatekeeper: Social interaction in interviews*. New York: Academic Press.

Espiritu, Y. L. (1992). *Asian American pan-ethnicity: Bridging institutions and identities*. Philadelphia: Temple University Press.

Ferguson, A. (2000). *Bad boys: Public schools in the making of black masculinity*. Ann Arbor: University of Michigan Press.

Fine, M. (1991). *Framing dropouts: Notes on the politics of an urban public high school*. Albany: State University of New York Press.

Fine, M. (1994). Working the hyphens: Reinventing self and other in qualitative research. In N. K. Denzin & Y. S. Lincoln (Eds.), *Handbook of qualitative research* (pp. 70–82). Thousand Oaks, CA: Sage.

Fong, T. P. (1994). *The first suburban Chinatown: The remaking of Monterey Park, California*. Philadelphia: Temple University Press.

Fordham, S. (1991). Peer-proofing academic competition among black adolescents: "Acting white" black American style. In C. E. Sleeter (Ed.), *Empowerment through multicultural education* (pp. 69–93). Albany: State University of New York Press.

Frankenberg, R. (1993). *White women, race matters: The social construction of whiteness*. Minneapolis: University of Minnesota Press.

Freire, E. (1986). *Education for critical consciousness*. New York: Continuum.

Friend, R. A. (1993). Choices, not closets: Heterosexism and homophobia in schools. In L. Weis & M. Fine (Eds.), *Beyond silenced voices. Class, race, and gender in United States schools* (pp. 209–235). Albany: State University of New York Press.

Fultz, M., & Brown, A. (2008). Historical perspectives on African American males as subjects of educational policy. *American Behavioral Scientist, 51*(7), 854–871.

Gibson, M. A. (1988). *Accommodation without assimilation: Sikh immigrants in an American high school*. Ithaca, NY: Cornell University Press.

Gibson, M. A. (1991). Ethnicity, gender and social class: The school adaptation patterns of West Indian youths. In M. A. Gibson & J. U. Ogbu (Eds.), *Minority status and schooling: A comparative study of immigrant and involuntary minorities* (pp. 169–203). New York: Garland.

Goffman, E. (1967). *Interaction ritual: Essays on face-to-face behavior*. New York: Pantheon.

Goldstein, B. (1985). *Schooling for cultural transitions: Hmong girls and boys in American high schools*. Unpublished doctoral dissertation, University of Wisconsin, Madison.

Hamamoto, D. (1992). The contemporary Asian American family on television. *Amerasia Journal, 18*(2), 35–53.

Harvey, D. (2005). *A brief history of neoliberalism*. Oxford: Oxford University Press.

Hayano, D. M. (1981). Ethnic identification and disidentification: Japanese-American views of Chinese-Americans. *Ethnic Groups, 3*(2), 157–171.

Hebdige, D. (1979). *Subculture: The meaning of style.* London: Methuen.

Hing, B. (1993). *Making and remaking Asian America through immigration policy, 1850–1990.* Stanford, CA: Stanford University Press.

Hirschman, C., & Wong, M. G. (1986). The extraordinary educational attainment of Asian Americans: A search for historical evidence and explanations. *Social Forces, 65*(1), 1–27.

Holtz, A. (1989). *Central High School. An ethnographic study of court-ordered female integration at a prestigious public high school.* Unpublished doctoral dissertation, University of Pennsylvania, Philadelphia.

Hsu, F. L. K. (1971). *The challenge of the American dream: The Chinese in the United States.* Belmont, CA: Wadsworth.

Hune, S. (1995). Rethinking race: Paradigms and policy formation. *Amerasia Journal, 21*(1 & 2), 29–40.

Hwang, S. (2005, November 19). The new white flight. *The Wall Street Journal.* Retrieved October 16, 2008, from http://online.wsj.com/article_email/SB113236377590902105-lMyQjAxMDE1MzEyOTMxNjkzWj.html

Islam, N. (2000). Research as an act of betrayal: Researching race in an Asian community in Los Angeles. In F. W. Twine & J. W. Warren (Eds.), *Racing research, researching race* (pp. 35–66). New York: New York University Press.

Jo, M. H. (1992). Korean merchants in the black community: Prejudice among the victims of prejudice. *Ethnic and Racial Studies, 15*(3), 395–411.

Katz, M. (1990). *The undeserving poor: From the war on poverty to the war on welfare.* New York: Pantheon.

Keyes, C. E. (1981). The dialectics of ethnic change. In C. E. Keyes (Ed.), *Ethnic change* (pp. 3–30). Seattle: University of Washington Press.

Kibria, N. (2000). Not Asian, black, or white? Reflections on South Asian American racial identity. In J. Wu & M. Song (Eds.), *Asian American studies: A reader* (pp. 247–254). New Brunswick, NJ: Rutgers University Press.

Kibria, N. (2002). *Becoming Asian American: Second-generation Chinese and Korean American identities.* Baltimore, MD: Johns Hopkins University Press.

Kim, C. (2000). *Bitter fruit: The politics of Black-Korean conflict in New York City.* New Haven, CT: Yale University Press.

Kim, E. H. (1993a). Home is where the ban is: A Korean American perspective on the Los Angeles upheavals. In R. Gooding-Williams (Ed.), *Reading Rodney King/reading urban uprising* (pp. 215–235). New York: Routledge.

Kim, E. H. (1993b). Preface. In J. Hagedorn (Ed.), *Charlie Chan is dead: An anthology of contemporary Asian American fiction* (pp. vii–xiv). New York: Penguin.

Kim, E.-Y. (1993). Career choice among second-generation Korean-Americans: Reflections of a cultural model of success. *Anthropology & Education Quarterly, 24*(3), 224–248.

Kitano, H. H. L. (1969). *Japanese Americans: The evolution of a subculture.* Englewood Cliffs, NJ: Prentice-Hall.

Kondo, D. K. (1990). *Crafting selves: Power, gender, and discourses of identity in a Japanese workplace.* Chicago: University of Chicago Press.

Kristoff, N. (2006, May 14). The model students. *New York Times*, pp. 4–13.

Kumashiro, K. K. (1999). Supplementing normalcy and otherness: Queer Asian American men reflect on stereotypes, identity, and oppression. *International Journal of Qualitative Studies in Education, 12*(5), 491–508.

Kumashiro, K. (2008). *The seduction of common sense: How the right has framed the debate on America's schools.* New York: Teachers College Press.

Kwong, P. (1987). *The new Chinatown.* New York: Hill & Wang.

Labaree, D. F. (1988). *The making of an American high school: The credentials market and the Central High School of Philadelphia, 1838–1939.* New Haven, CT: Yale University Press.

Lareau, A. (2003). *Unequal childhoods: Class, race, and family life.* Berkeley: University of California Press.

Lather, P. (1986). Research as praxis. *Harvard Educational Review, 56*(3), 257–277.

Lee, J. F. J. (1991). *Asian Americans.* New York: New Press.

Lee, S. J. (2005). *Up against whiteness: Race, school, and immigrant youth.* New York: Teachers College Press.

Lee, S. J., & Kumashiro, K. (2005). *A report on the status of Asian Americans and Pacific Islanders in education: Beyond the "model minority" stereotype.* Washington, DC: National Education Association.

Lee, S. M. (1989). Asian American immigration and American race-relations: From exclusion to acceptance? *Ethnic & Racial Studies, 12*(2), 368–390.

Lee, S. S. (2006). Over-represented and de-minoritized: The racialization of Asian Americans in higher education. *InterActions: UCLA Journal of Education and Information Studies, 2*(2), Article 4. Available at http://repositories.cdlib.org/gseis/interactions/vol2/iss2/art4

Lee, Y. (1991). Korean in Japan and the United States. In M. A. Gibson & J. U. Ogbu (Eds.), *Minority status and schooling: A comparative study of immigrant and involuntary minorities* (pp. 131–167). New York: Garland.

Lei, J. (2003). (Un)Necessary toughness?: Those "loud black girls" and those "quiet Asian boys." *Anthropology & Education Quarterly, 34*(2), 158–181.

Lew, J. (2006). *Asian Americans in class: Charting the achievement gap among Korean American youth.* New York: Teachers College Press.

Li, G. (2002). *"East is East, West is West"? Home literacy, culture, and schooling.* New York: Peter Lang.

Li, G. (2005). Other people's success: Impact of the "model minority" myth on underachieving Asian students in North America. *KEDI Journal of Educational Policy, 2*(1), 69–86.

Li, G., & Wang, L. (Eds.). (2008). *Model minority myth revisited: An interdisciplinary approach to demystifying Asian American educational experiences.* Charlotte, NC: Information Age Publishing.

Lie, J. (2004). The Black-Asian conflict? In G. Frederickson & N. Foner (Eds.), *Not just black and white* (pp. 301–314). New York: Russell Sage.

Light, I., & Bonacich, E. (1988). *Immigrant entrepreneurs: Koreans in Los Angeles, 1965–1982.* Berkeley: University of California Press.

Lipman, P. (2004). *High stakes education: Inequality, globalization, and urban school reform.* New York: Routledge.

Lipman, P. (2008). Mixed-income schools and housing: Advancing the neoliberal agenda. *Journal of Education Policy, 23*(2), 119–134.

Lipman, P., & Hursh, D. (2007). Renaissance 2010: The reassertion of ruling-class power through Neoliberal policies in Chicago. *Policy Futures in Education, 5*(2), 160–178.

Lopez, N. (2003). *Hopeful girls, troubled boys: Race and gender disparity in urban education.* New York: Routledge.

Louie, V. (2004). *Compelled to excel: Immigration, education, and opportunity among Chinese Americans.* Stanford, CA: Stanford University Press.

Lowe, L. (1991). Heterogeneity, hybridity, multiplicity: Marking Asian American differences. *Diaspora, 1*(1), 24–44.

Maira, S. (2001). *Desis in the house: Indian American youth in New York City.* Philadelphia: Temple University Press.

Mark, D. M. L., & Chih, G. (1982). *A place called America.* Dubuque, IA: Kendall Hunt.

Matsuda, M. (1991). *Voices of America: Accent, antidiscrimination law, and jurisprudence for the last reconstruction,* 100 Yale L.J. 1329

Matute-Bianchi, M. E. (1986). Ethnic identities and patterns of school success and failure among Mexican-descent and Japanese-American students in a California high school: An ethnographic analysis. *American Journal of Education, 95*(1), 233–255.

Matute-Bianchi, M. E. (1991). Situational ethnicity and patterns of school performance among immigrant and nonimmigrant Mexican-descent students. In M. A. Gibson & J. U. Ogbu (Eds.), *Minority status and schooling: A comparative study of immigrant and involuntary minorities* (pp. 205–247). New York: Garland Publishing.

McGinnis, T. (2007). "Khmer pride": Being and becoming Khmer-American in an urban migrant program. *Journal of Southeast Asian American Education & Advancement, 2.* Retrieved October 15, 2008, from http://jsaaea.coehd.utsa.edu/index.php/JSAAEA/issue/view/5

McLaren, P. (1982). "Bein' tough": Rituals of resistance in the culture of working-class schoolgirls. *Canadian Woman Studies, 4*(1), 20–24.

McLaren, P. (1991). Decentering culture: Postmodernism, resistance, and critical pedagogy. In N. B. Wyner (Ed.), *Current perspectives on the culture of schools* (pp. 232–257). Boston: Brookline.

McNeil, L. (2000). *Contradictions of school reform: Educational costs of standardized testing.* New York: Routledge.

McRobbie, A. (1978). Working class girls and the culture of femininity. In Women's Studies Group, Centre for Contemporary Cultural Studies, University of Birmingham (Eds.), *Women take issue* (pp. 96–108). London: Hutchinson.

Melendy, H. B. (1977). *Asians in America: Filipinos, Koreans, and East Indians.* Boston: Twayne.

Menken, K. (2008). *English learners left behind: Standardized testing as language policy.* Tonawanda, NY: Multilingual Matters.

Min, P. (1991). Cultural and economic boundaries of Korean ethnicity: A comparative analysis. *Ethnic and Racial Studies, 14*(2), 225–241.

Min, P. (1998). *Changes and conflicts: Korean immigrant families in New York.* Boston: Allyn & Bacon.

Mordkowitz, E. R., & Ginsberg, H. P. (1987). Early academic socialization of successful Asian-American college students. *Quarterly Newsletter of the Laboratory of Comparative Human Cognition, 9*(2), 85–91.

Morrison, T. (1992). Introduction: Friday on Potomac. In T. Morrison (Ed.), *Race-ing justice, en-gendering power: Essays on Anita Hill, Clarence Thomas, and the construction of social reality* (pp. vii–xxx). New York: Pantheon.

Newman, K. S. (1993). *Declining fortunes: The withering of the American dream*. New York: Basic Books.

Ngo, B., & Lee, S. J. (2007). Complicating the image of model minority success: A review of Southeast Asian American education. *Review of Educational Research, 77*(4), 415–453.

Oakes, J. (1985). *Keeping track: How schools structure inequality*. New Haven, CT: Yale University Press.

O'Connor, C. (1997). Dispositions toward (collective) struggle and educational resilience in the inner city: A case analysis of six African American high school students. *American Educational Research Journal, 34*(4), 593–629.

Ogbu, J. U. (1978). *Minority education and caste: The American system in cross-cultural perspective*. New York: Academic.

Ogbu, J. U. (1983). Minority status and schooling in plural societies. *Comparative Education Review, 27*(2), 168–190.

Ogbu, J. U. (1987). Variability in minority school performance: A problem in search of an explanation. *Anthropology & Education Quarterly, 18*(4), 312–334.

Ogbu, J. U. (1989). The individual in collective adaptation: A framework for focusing on academic underperformance and dropping out among involuntary minorities. In L. Weis, E. Farrar, & H. G. Petrie (Eds.), *Dropouts from school: Issues, dilemmas, and solutions* (pp. 181–204). Albany: State University of New York Press.

Ogbu, J. U. (1990). Minority education in comparative perspective. *Journal of Negro Education, 59*(1), 45–57.

Ogbu, J. U. (1991). Immigrant and involuntary minorities in comparative perspective. In M. Gibson & J. U. Ogbu (Eds.), *Minority status and schooling: A comparative study of immigrant and involuntary minorities* (pp. 3–33). New York: Garland.

Ogbu, J. U. (1994). Racial stratification and education in the United States: Why inequality persists. *Teachers College Record, 96*(2), 265–298.

Okamoto, D. (2003, December). Toward a theory of pan-ethnicity: Explaining Asian American collective action. *American Sociological Review, 68*, 811–842.

Okihiro, G. (1994). *Margins and mainstreams: Asians in American history and culture*. Seattle: University of Washington Press.

Olsen, L. (1997). *An invisible crisis: The educational needs of Asian Pacific American Youth*. New York: Asian Americans/Pacific Islanders in Philanthropy.

Omi, M., & Winant, H. (1986). *Racial formation in the United States: From the 1960s to the 1980s*. New York: Routledge.

Ong, P. (1999). Proposition 209 and its implications. In P. Ong (Eds.), *Impacts of affirmative action: Policies and consequences in California* (pp. 197–209). Walnut Creek, CA: Altamira.

Osajima, K. (1988). Asian Americans as the model minority: An analysis of the popular press image in the 1960s and 1980s. In G. Y. Okihiro, S. Hune, A. A. Hansen, & J. M. Liu (Eds.), *Reflections on shattered windows. Promises and prospects for Asian American studies* (pp. 165–174). Pullman: Washington State University Press.

Palumbo-Liu, D. (1994). Los Angeles, Asians, and perverse ventriloquisms: On the functions of Asian America in the recent American imaginary. *Public Culture, 6*(2), 365–381.

Pang, V. O. (1990). Asian American children: A diverse population. *The Educational Forum, 55*(1), 49–65.

Pang, V. O., & Cheng, L. (Eds.). (1998). *Struggling to be heard: The unmet needs of Asian Pacific American children*. Albany: State University of New York Press.

Pang, V. O., Kiang, P., & Pak, Y. (2003). Asian Pacific American students: Challenging a biased educational system. In J. Banks (Ed.), *Handbook of research on multicultural education* (2nd ed., pp. 542–563). San Francisco, CA: Jossey Bass.

Park, C., Goodwin, A. L., & Lee, S. J. (Eds.). (2001). *Research on the education of Asian and Pacific Americans*. Greenwich, CT: Information Age Publishing.

Park, C., Goodwin, A. L., & Lee, S. J. (Eds.). (2003). *Asian American identities, families and schooling*. Greenwich, CT: Information Age Publishing.

Park, C., Endo, R., Lee, S. J., & Rong, X. L. (Eds.). (2007). *Asian American education: Acculturation, literacy development, and learning*. Greenwich, CT: Information Age Publishing.

Park, E., & Park, S. (1999). A new American dilemma? Asian Americans and Latinos in race theorizing. *Journal of Asian American Studies, 2*(3), 289–309.

Park, G. C. (2007). *Racialized Americanization: Schooling, peer, and Korean immigrant youth in urban school*. Unpublished doctoral dissertation, Department of Educational Policy Studies, University of Wisconsin–Madison.

Park, K. (1996). Use and abuse of race and culture: Black-Korean tension in America. *American Anthropologist, 98*(3), 492–499.

Park, K. (1997). *The Korean American dream: Immigrants and small business in New York City*. Ithaca, NY: Cornell University Press.

Park, S. (2004). "Korean American Evangelical": A resolution of sociological ambivalence among Korean American college students. In T. Carnes & F. Yang (Eds.), *Asian American religions: The making and remaking of borders and boundaries* (pp. 182–204). New York: New York University Press.

Perry, P. (2002). *Shades of white: White kids and racial identities in high school*. Durham, NC: Duke University Press.

Peters, H. A. (1988). *A study of Southeast Asian youth in Philadelphia: A final report*. Washington, DC: U.S. Department of Health and Human Services, Office of Refugee Resettlement.

Philips, S. U. (1983). *The invisible culture: Communication in classroom and community on the Warm Springs Indian Reservation*. New York: Longman.

Phinney, J. S. (1989). Stages of ethnic identity development in minority group adolescents. *Journal of Early Adolescence, 9*(1 & 2), 34–49.

Reeves, T., & Bennett, C. (2003, March). *The Asian American and Pacific Islander population in the United States* (Current Population Reports). Washington, DC: U.S. Census Bureau.

Reeves, T., & Bennett, C. (2004, December). *We the people: Asians in the United States* (Census 2000 Special Reports). Washington, DC: U.S. Census Bureau.

Reyes, A. (2007). *Language, identity, and stereotype among Southeast Asian American youth.* Mahwah, NJ: Lawrence Erlbaum.

Rizvi, E. (1993). Children and the grammar of popular racism. In C. McCarthy & W. Crichlow (Eds.), *Race, identity, and representation in education* (pp. 126–139). New York: Routledge.

Robbins, C. (2004, September). Racism and the authority of neoliberalism: A review of three new books on the persistence of racial inequality in a color-blind era. *Journal for Critical Education Policy, 2*(2). Available at http://www.jceps.com/?pageID=article&articleID=35

Robles, R. (2006). *Asian Americans and the shifting politics of race: The dismantling of affirmative action at an elite public high school.* New York: Routledge.

Roman, L. G. (1993). White is a color! White defensiveness, postmodernism, and anti-racist pedagogy. In C. McCarthy & W. Crichlow (Eds.), *Race, identity, and representation in education* (pp. 71–88). New York: Routledge.

Roman, L. G., & Apple, M. W. (1990). Is naturalism a move away from positivism? Materialist and feminist approaches to subjectivity in ethnographic research. In E. W. Eisner & A. Peshkin (Eds.), *Qualitative inquiry in education: The continuing debate* (pp. 38–73). New York: Teachers College Press.

Rosenbloom, S., & Way, N. (2004). Experiences of discrimination among African American, Asian American, and Latino adolescents in an urban high school. *Journal of Youth & Society, 35,* 420–451.

Rudrappa, S. (2004). *Ethnic routes to becoming American: Indian immigrants and the cultures of citizenship.* New Brunswick, NJ: Rutgers University Press.

Rumbaut, R. G., & Weeks, J. R. (1986). Fertility and adaptation: Indochinese refugees in the United Stares. *International Migration Review, 20*(2), 428–466.

Sandhu, S. (2004). Instant karma: The commercialization of Asian Indian culture. In J. Lee & M. Zhou (Eds.), *Asian American youth: Culture, identity, and ethnicity* (pp. 131–141). New York: Routledge.

Sarroub, L. (2005). *All American Yemeni Girls: Being Muslim in a public school.* Philadelphia: University of Pennsylvania Press.

Schneider, B., & Lee, Y. (1990). A model for academic success: The school and home environment of East Asian students. *Anthropology & Education Quarterly, 21*(4), 358–377.

Siu, S. F. (1992). *Toward an understanding of Chinese-American educational achievement* (Report No. 2). Boston: Wheelock College, Center on Families, Communities, Schools, and Children's Learning.

Sleeter, C. E. (1993). How white teachers construct race. In C. McCarthy & W. Crichlow (Eds.), *Race, identity, and representation in education* (pp. 157–171). New York: Routledge.

Smith-Hefner, N. (1999). *Khmer American: Identity and moral education in a diasporic community.* Berkeley: University of California Press.

Solomon, R. P. (1992). *Black resistance to high school: Forging a separatist culture.* Albany: State University of New York Press.

Suárez-Orozco, C., & Suárez-Orozco, M. M. (2001). *Children of immigration.* Cambridge, MA: Harvard University Press.

Suárez-Orozco, M. M. (1989). *Central American refugees and U.S. high schools: A psychological study of motivation and achievement*. Stanford, CA: Stanford University Press.

Suárez-Orozco, M. M. (1991). Immigrant adaptation to schooling: A Hispanic case. In M. A. Gibson & J. U. Ogbu (Eds.), *Minority status and schooling: A comparative study of immigrant and involuntary minorities* (pp. 37–61). New York: Garland Publishing.

Success story of one minority group in the U.S. (1966, December 26). *U.S. News & World Report*, pp. 73–78.

Sue, S., & Kitano, H. H. L. (1973). Stereotypes as a measure of success. *Journal of Social Issues, 29*(2), 83–98.

Sue, S., & Okazaki, S. (1990). Asian-American educational achievements: A phenomenon in search of an explanation. *American Psychologist, 45*(8), 913–920.

Sue, S., & Sue, D. W. (1971). Chinese-American personality and mental health. *Amerasia Journal, 1*(2), 36–49.

Sung, B. L. (1987). *The adjustment experience of Chinese immigrant children in New York City*. New York: Center for Migration Studies.

Suzuki, R. H. (1980). Education and the socialization of Asian Americans: A revisionist analysis of the "model minority" thesis. In R. Endo, S. Sue, & N. N. Wagner (Eds.), *Asian Americans: Social and psychological perspectives* (Vol. 2, pp. 155–175). Ben Lomond, CA: Science and Behavior Books.

Takagi, D. Y. (1992). *The retreat from race: Asian American admissions and racial politics*. New Brunswick, NJ: Rutgers University Press.

Takagi, D. Y. (1994). Maiden voyage: Excursion into sexuality and identity politics in Asian America. *Amerasia Journal, 20*(1), 1–17.

Takaki, R. (1989). *Strangers from a different shore: A history of Asian Americans*. New York: Penguin.

Thao, P. (1998). *Mong education at the crossroads*. Lanham, MD: Rowman & Littlefield.

Trottier, R. (1981). Charters of pan-ethnic identity: Indigenous American Indians and immigrant Asian-Americans. In C. E. Keyes (Ed.), *Ethnic change* (pp. 271–305). Seattle: University of Washington Press.

Trueba, H. T., Cheng, L., & Ima, K. (1993). *Myth or reality: Adaptive strategies of Asian Americans in California*. Washington, DC: Falmer.

Tuan, M. (1998). *Forever foreigners or honorary whites?: The Asian ethnic experience today*. New Brunswick, NJ: Rutgers University Press.

Tyson, K. (2002). Weighing in: Elementary-age students and the debate on attitudes toward school among black students. *Social Forces, 80*(4), 1157–1189.

Um, K. (2003). *A dream denied: Educational experiences of Southeast Asian American youth: Issues and recommendations*. Washington, DC: Southeast Asia Resource Action Center.

U.S. Census Bureau. (2007). *The American community—Asians: 2004* (American Community Survey Reports). Retrieved July 22, 2008, from http://www.census.gov/prod/2007pubs/acs-05.pdf

Valenzuela, A. (1999). *Subtractive schooling: U.S.-Mexican youth and the politics of caring*. Albany: State University of New York Press.

Vaught, S. (2008). Writing against racism: Telling white lies and reclaiming culture. *Qualitative Inquiry 14*(4), 566–589.

Verma, R. (2008). *Backlash: South Asian immigrant youth on the margins.* Rotterdam, The Netherlands: Sense Publishers.

Walker-Moffat, W. (1995). *The other side of the Asian American success story.* San Francisco, CA: Jossey Bass.

Wang, L. L. (2008). Myths and realities of Asian American success: Reassessing and redefining the "model minority" stereotype. In G. Li & W. Wang (Eds.), *Model minority myth revisited: An interdisciplinary approach to demystifying Asian American educational experiences* (pp. 21–42). Charlotte, NC: Information Age Publishing.

Waters, M. C. (1990). *Ethnic options. Choosing identities in America.* Berkeley: University of California Press.

Waters, M. (1999). *Black identities: West Indian immigrant dreams and American realities.* Cambridge, MA: Harvard University Press.

Watkins, M. (1994). *On the real side: Laughing, lying, and signifying.* New York: Simon & Schuster.

Wei, W. (2004). A commentary on young Asian American activists from the 1960s to the present. In J. Lee & M. Zhou (Eds.), *Asian American youth: Culture, identity and ethnicity* (pp. 299–312). New York: Routledge.

Weinberg, M. (1997). *Asian-American education: Historical background and current realities.* Mahwah, NJ: Lawrence Erlbaum Associates.

Weis, L. (1990). *Working class without work: High school students in a deindustrializing economy.* New York: Routledge.

Wellman, D. T. (1977). *Portraits of white racism.* Cambridge, UK: Cambridge University Press.

West, C. (1992). Black leadership and the pitfalls of racial reasoning. In T. Morrison (Ed.), *Race-ing justice, engendering power. Essays on Anita Hill, Clarence Thomas, and the construction of social reality* (pp. 390–401). New York: Pantheon.

Whitty, G. (1997). Creating quasi-markets in education: A review of recent research on parental choice and school autonomy in three countries. *Review of Research in Education, 22,* 3–47.

Williams, P. J. (1991). *The alchemy of race and rights.* Cambridge, MA: Harvard University Press.

Willis, P. E. (1977). *Learning to labor: How working class kids get working class jobs.* New York: Columbia University Press.

Wong, L. M. (1993, November). *Shifting identities and fixing hierarchies. Whiteness and the myth of the model minority.* Paper presented at the annual meeting of the American Education Studies Association, Chicago.

Wong, M. G. (1980, October). Model students? Teachers' perceptions and expectations of their Asian and White students. *Sociology of Education, 53,* 236–246.

Wong, N. W. A. (2008). *"They are like a bridge": An ethnographic case study of a community-based youth center.* Unpublished doctoral dissertation, Department of Educational Policy Studies, University of Wisconsin–Madison.

Wu, F. (1995, Summer). Neither black nor white: Asian Americans and affirmative action. *Boston College Third World Law Journal, 15,* 225–284.

Wu, F. (2002). *Yellow: Race in America beyond black and white.* New York: Basic Books.

Zhou, M., & Bankston, C. (1998). *Growing up American: The adaptation of Vietnamese adolescents in the United States.* New York: Russell Sage.

Zhou, M., & Kim, R. (2006). The paradox of ethnicization and assimilation: The development of ethnic organizations in the Chinese immigrant community in the United States. In K. P. Eng & E. Hu-DeHart (Eds.), *Voluntary organizations in the Chinese diaspora* (pp. 231–252). Hong Kong: Hong Kong University Press.

Index

About the Author

Stacey J. Lee is Professor of Educational Policy Studies at the University of Wisconsin–Madison. Her research focuses on the influences of race, class, gender, and local context on educational experiences of immigrant youth. She is the author of *Up Against Whiteness: Race, School, and Immigrant Youth*, published by Teachers College Press.